INFORMATION

Editorial office
Octane, 1 Tower Court, Irchester Road,
Wollaston, Northants NN29 7PJ, UK
Tel: +44 (0)207 907 6585. Fax: +44 (0)1933 663367
Email: info@octane-magazine.com
Website: www.octane-magazine.com

Advertising office
Octane Media Advertising Dept, 19 Highfield Lane,
Maidenhead, Berkshire SL6 3AN, UK
Tel: +44 (0)1628 510080. Fax: +44 (0)1628 510090
Email: ads@octane-magazine.com

Managing editor:	David Lillywhite
Art editor:	Rob Gould
Production:	Sarah Bradley
	Mark Dixon
Advertising director:	Sanjay Seetanah
Advertising sales:	Rob Schulp
Advertising production:	Anisha Mogra
	Kerem Kolcak
Publisher	Geoff Love
Newstrade director	Martin Belson
Marketing manager	Juliette Cooper
Managing director	Ian Westwood
Group finance director	Ian Leggett
COO	Brett Reynolds
CEO	James Tye
Chairman	Felix Dennis

Licensing
To license this product, please contact Winnie Liesenfeld on +44 (0)20 7907 6134 or email winnie_liesenfeld@dennis.co.uk

Magbook

The Magbook brand is a trademark of Dennis Publishing Ltd.

Classics in Camera is published under licence from Octane Media Ltd, a subsidiary company of Dennis Publishing Limited, United Kingdom. All rights in the licensed material belong to Felix Dennis, Octane Media or Dennis Publishing and may not be reproduced, whether in whole or in part, without their prior written consent. Octane is a registered trademark.

Repro by Octane Repro
Printed by BGP, Bicester
Distribution by Seymour, 2 East Poultry Avenue, London EC1A 9PT. Tel: +44 (0)20 7429 4000

Periodicals Postage paid @ Emigsville, PA. Postmaster: send address corrections to Octane Media c/o 3330 Pacific Ave, Suite 404, Virginia Beach, VA 23451

Classics in Camera is published by Octane Media Ltd.

The publisher makes every effort to ensure the magazine's contents are correct. All material published in Classics in Camera is copyright and unauthorised reproduction is forbidden. The editors and publishers of this magazine give no warranties, guarantees or assurances and make no representations regarding any goods or services advertised in this edition.

Dennis Publishing (UK) Ltd uses a layered Privacy Notice, giving you brief details about how we would like to use your personal information. For full details please visit our website www.dennis.co.uk/privacy/ or call us on 0844 844 0053. If you have any questions, please ask, as submitting your details indicates your consent, until you choose otherwise, that we and our partners may contact you about products and services that will be of relevance to you via direct mail, phone, e-mail and SMS. You can opt-out at ANY time via www.subsinfo.co.uk or privacy@dennis.co.uk or 0844 844 0053.

editorial

A WHOLE WORLD OF EXCITEMENT

Can there be a better subject for photography than classic cars? It's not just the variety of shapes and sizes they offer, or the way the light catches those remarkable curves, it's also the excitement and glamour of the classic car world. Fascinating people, beautiful women, amazing locations. We've got it all!

Classics in Camera takes some of the best pictures from six years of *Octane*, the magazine that's renowned for its superb photography by some of the best practitioners of the art.

There are perfectly composed studio pictures, hair-raising action shots, reportage-style people pics... Most of all, there are wonderful, wonderful cars, from pre-war leviathans to the latest supercars.

I love the sheer bravery portrayed in the long-distance historic rally car pictures (Libyan desert in a 1908 chain-driven Itala, anyone?) and the intensity of the supercar action photography, taken by intrepid photographers hanging out of the camera car just inches from the tarmac.

Enjoy – and remember that there's more of the same every month in *Octane* magazine and on www.octane-magazine.com.

> Perfectly composed studio pictures, hair-raising action shots – and most of all, wonderful, wonderful cars

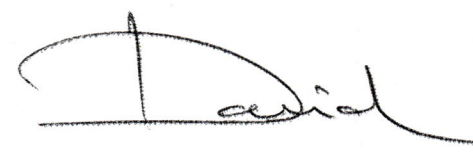

David Lillywhite, managing editor

CLASSICS IN CAMERA

McLaren F1 GTR
PAUL HARMER

To celebrate its 50th issue, *Octane* asked 50 'players' in the historics world for their all-time favourite car. The McLaren F1 won hands down, and this is *Octane* columnist and Pink Floyd drummer Nick Mason's ex-Le Mans GTR – here driven by Nick himself.

CLASSICS IN CAMERA

Ferrari 288GTO
GEORGE BAMFORD

It's one of the most exciting Ferraris ever – and yet its elegant Pininfarina looks have ironically left the 288GTO in the bolder F40's shadow. But with 400bhp, a 190mph top speed and 0-60mph in 4.7 seconds, the 288 gives little away to its younger sibling.

CLASSICS IN CAMERA 7

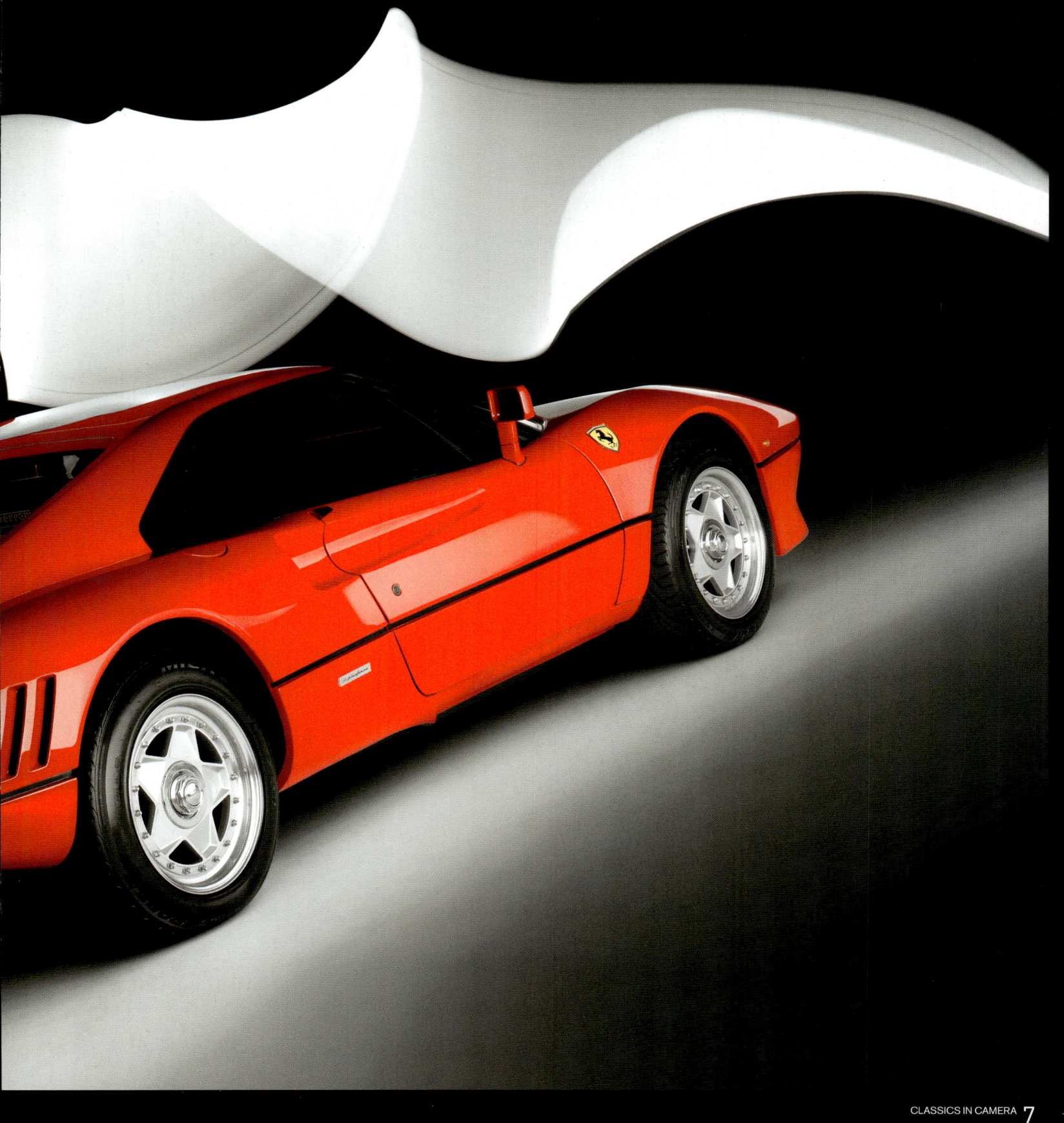

Rover-BRM
JOHN COLLEY

Rover was one of the world's most innovative auto makers in the 1950s and '60s. The 1963 Rover-BRM Le Mans car was powered by a gas turbine and ran in the '63 and '65 races, finishing 10th overall in the latter. It was also tested on public roads by *Motor* magazine...

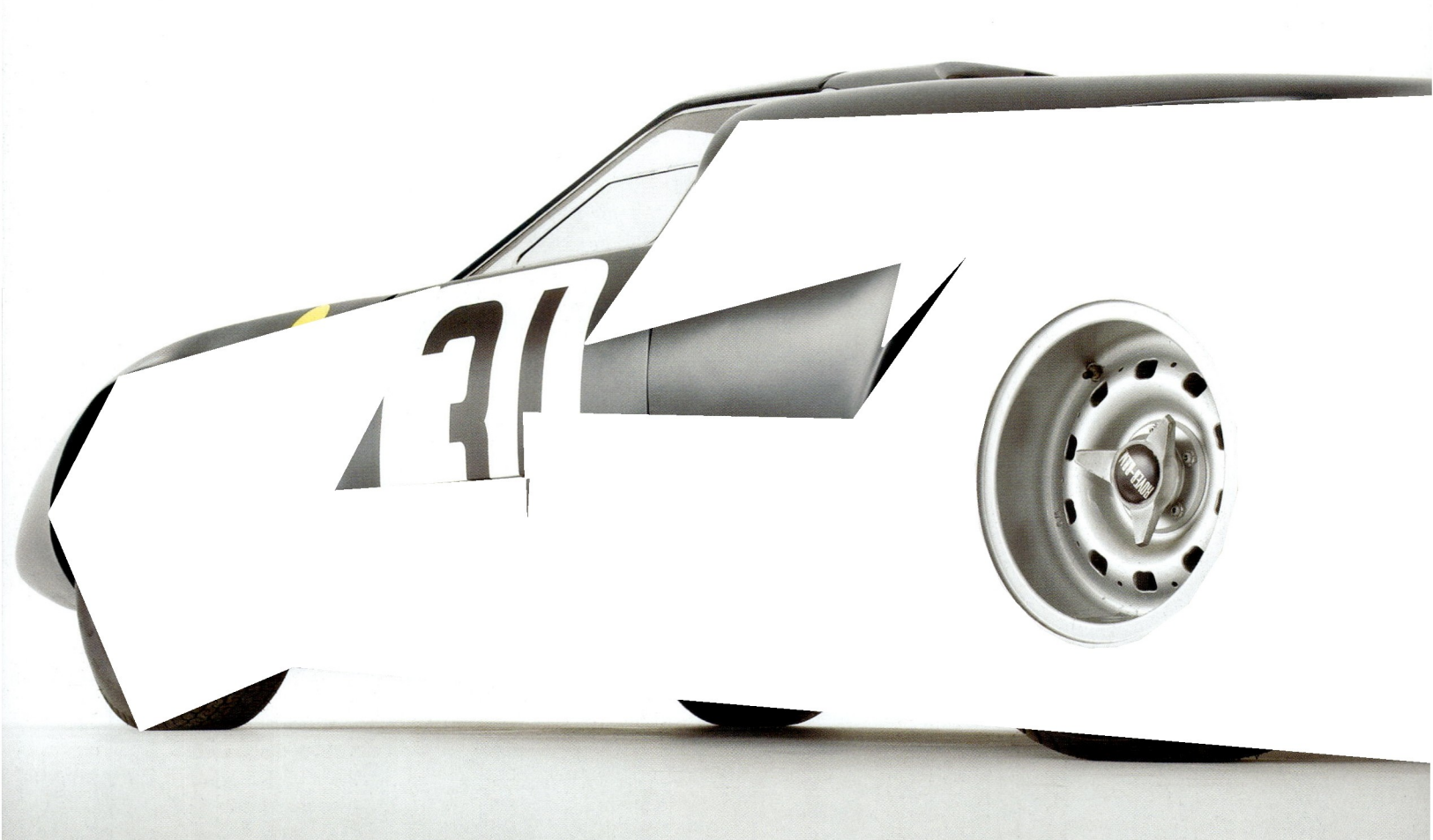

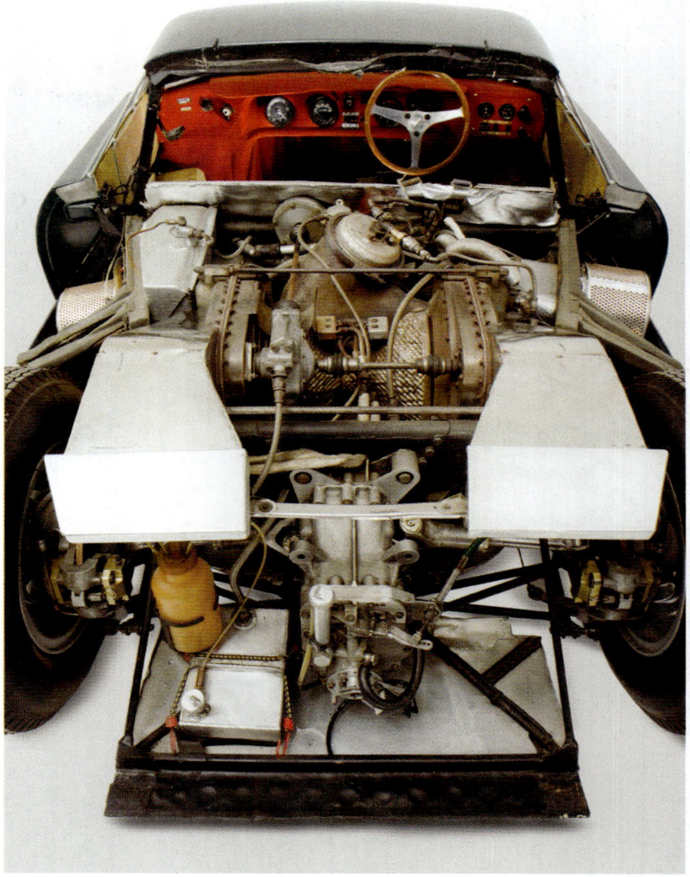

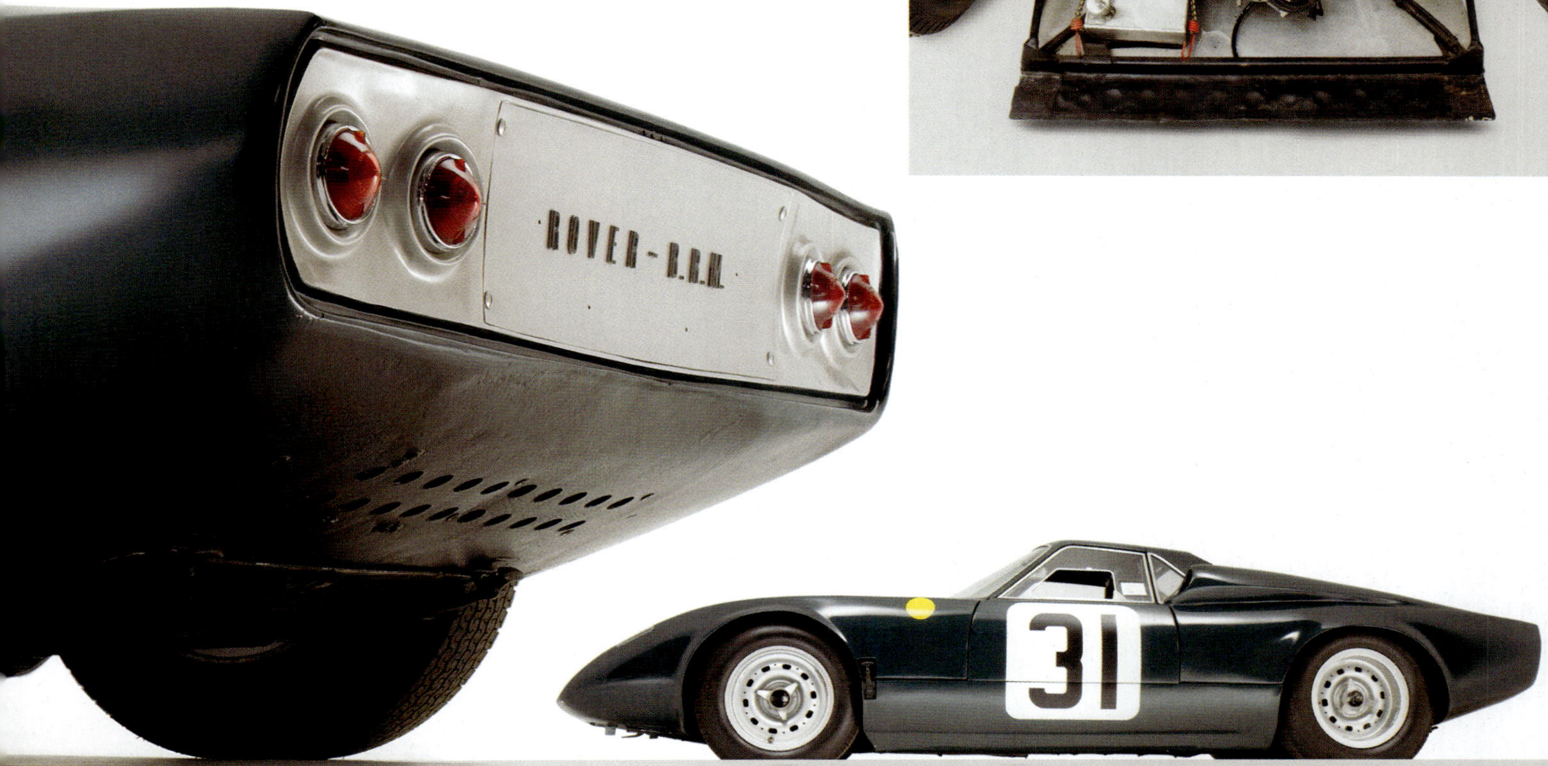
ROVER - B.R.M.
31

CLASSICS IN CAMERA

AC 427 S/C
MARK DIXON
This 427 visited Brooklands along with one of every Cobra variant for an all-encompassing *Octane* feature. It was built by AC Heritage at Brooklands in 2001, using a period-correct tubular chassis and an aluminium body shaped over tooling from the AC factory at Thames Ditton.

Hawk Cars

the collection...

...a motoring icon may be closer to reality than you ever thought

F.I.A

427

289

Workshop

Talon Sportscars Ltd
Official Build Agents for Hawk Cars
www.talonsportscars.com
E: enquiries@talonsportscars.com
T: 01509 842740

HF 2000/3000

For the ultimate in authenticity, quality & engineering integrity

All parts available for original 289 & 427 cars

Supplier of coffin spoke and FIA Mk2 & Mk3 427 wheels

Tel: 01892 750341 / 750282
Oakdene, Riverhall Hill, Frant, East Sussex TN3 9EP
gerry@hawkcars.co.uk
www.hawkcars.co.uk

KIRKHAM motorsports

CLASSICS IN CAMERA

Jaguar XK150 3.8S
MICHAEL BAILIE
Ultimate version of Jaguar's fabled XK grand tourers was the 3.8-litre XK150 in 'S' spec, which produced a claimed 265bhp (in reality more like 200bhp). It also had wind-up windows and a padded dashboard – luxury in 1960!

Steve McQueen's 911
MATTHEW HOWELL

McQueen liked the slate-grey Porsche 911 used in the filming of *Le Mans* so much that he had it shipped back to Los Angeles. It's now owned by an enthusiast who bought it for a song in 2005, just before prices for all things Steve went stratospheric...

RS
ROAD SCHOLARS

Graduate

Work

Work

Work

Promotion

Work

Work

Work

Wife & kids

Work

Work

Work

REWARD

Sales • Purchasing • Restoration
Everything for the discerning Porsche collector
TheAirCooledGuys.com • 919.854.2277

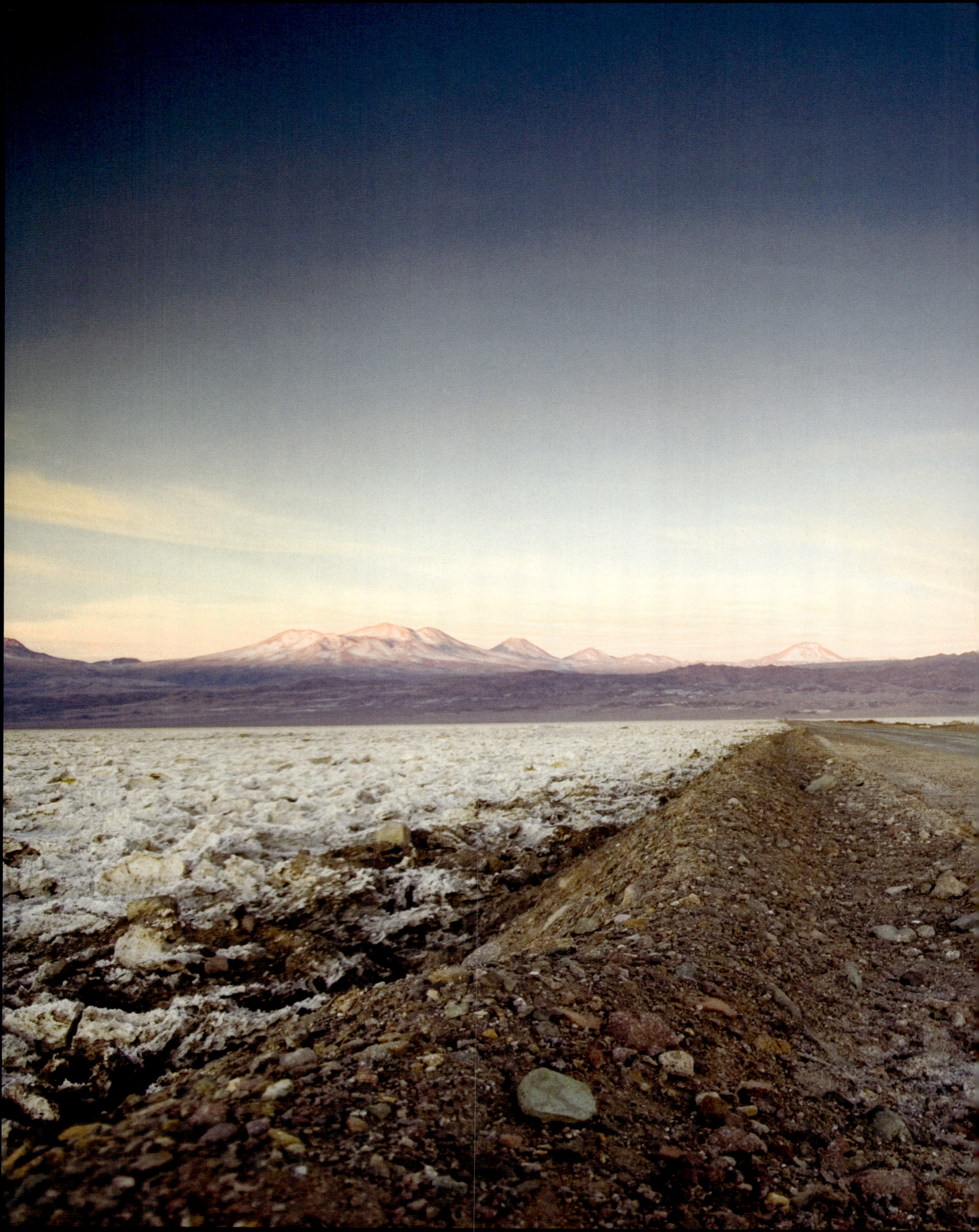

Ferrari 599GTB
TOM SALT

Never a company to do things by halves, Ferrari staged a 20,000-mile promotional drive across South America with two 599GTB Fioranos in 2006. The £180k luxury supercars despatched the rough roads in Chile and Bolivia with ease, running on Pirelli rally-spec tyres.

'Bloody Mary'
TOM WOOD

Created by two 1920s schoolboy brothers using only hand tools, this motorcycle-engined 'Shelsley special' became a formidable giant-killer on pre-war sprint and hillclimb courses. One of the brothers, John Bolster, later wrote that it was '…built with the object of driving around a field as dangerously as possible!'

JSW Group Ltd.

1961 - Ferrari 156 F1 "sharknose" recreation

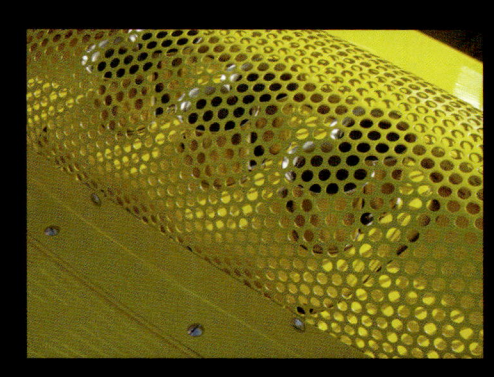

Alfa Romeo - Lancia - Ferrari - Maserati - Aston Martin - Jaguar - Mercedes - Bentley - Rolls Royce

e info@jswl.co.uk
t +44 (0)2392 254488
f +44 (0)2392 254489
w www.jimstokes.co.uk
a 7/8 Pipers Wood Industrial Park, Waterlooville, Hants., PO7 7XU, UK.

in association with:

ben
the automotive industry charity

Polygon
International Vehicle
Transportation Ltd.

Ladies' man
GP LIVE
Eighty years young, Sir Stirling Moss has always had a eye for the fairer sex – and what better way to prepare for on-track action than in the company of a beautiful woman?

Girls, girls, girls!
STEVE HAVELOCK / JOHN COLLEY / DAVID CORFIELD

Whether it's weapon-toting Bond minxes and funky 1960s chicks at the Goodwood Festival of Speed, or a bikini-clad supporter at America's inaugural Bullrun, no motor sport event would be complete without girls!

CLASSICS IN CAMERA

Ferrari Daytona
GEORGE BAMFORD

Ferrari's 365GTB/4 Daytona is the archetypal front-engined V12 Ferrari, though more often found in 'retail red' than this dramatic Giallo Fly (yellow) shade. Always an extremely desirable car, it's widely regarded as a bellwether for the ebb and flow of classic car values.

Auto Union Type D
MATTHEW HOWELL

Hidden from the outside world, two UK companies secretly built a recreation of the final incarnation of the legendary pre-war Auto Union racers – and the 1939 Type D V12-engined machine was exclusively revealed in *Octane* on its 2005 debut.

SWISS WAXMAKERS SINCE 1930

SWISSVAX™
HIGH PERFORMANCE CAR CARE
HAND MADE IN SWITZERLAND
WWW.SWISSVAX.COM

CARE FOR YOUR DREAM™

Swissvax is a uniquely handcrafted car care system made in Switzerland and designed to be the finest product line of automotive cosmetic maintenance in the world. Since 1930, the Anwander family has been creating magnificent Carnauba wax formulations. The Swissvax system comprises two major components: a cleaning pre-wax oil which prepares and nourishes the surface, followed by the wax formulation of your choice. The essential oils found in Swissvax waxes including avocado, passion fruit and orange produce a wonderfully aromatic fragrance, combined with high volumes of pure Brazilian carnauba, the world's purest, hardest and most transparent natural wax. These exclusive formulas are very easy to apply, leaving no white residue or wax build-up. There are, quite simply, no compromises when it comes to our pursuit of the ultimate wax and car care system. No wonder **Swissvax is OEM to Rolls-Royce Motorcars, Mercedes-Benz Classic, Spyker Cars, Lamborghini and Bugatti.** We invite you to see for yourself what delighted enthusiasts and collectors all over the world are discovering about Swissvax.

Swissvax «Saphir»
Premium wax with over 40% by vol. of Brazilian Carnauba and an excellent choice for modern water based paints.
Price: **£80.00**

Swissvax «Shield»
Natural wax **with PTFE** for a legendary «non-stick» effect of dirt and insects. Our best-selling formula for German Autobahns.
Price: **£90.00**

Swissvax «Glacier»
Premium wax for white cars only. It's highly dirt repellent formulation works to minimise the effect and appearance of «black run marks» after rain. Price: **£80.00**

Swissvax «Best of Show»
Our famous concours wax with 50% by vol. of pure Brazilian Carnauba for a deep, wet «show car» shine.
Price: **£135.00**

Swissvax «Mystery»
The company's founder own formula with 55% by vol. of pure white Carnauba achieves a shine that goes beyond the word «shiny». Price: **£335.00**

Paul Dalton's «Crystal Rock»
State-of-the-Art-wax with 76% by wax vol. of pure Brazilian ivory carnauba wax. It coats a cars paintwork in a smooth and glossy, yet tough and protective, water-repellent film. Price: **£500.00**

First application requires a wax pretreatment with «Cleaner Fluid» or Swissvax waxes will not adhere to the paint surface. Price: **£25.00**

Swissvax «Master Collection»
The complete valet kit for your car will enhance every detail of your automobile to award winning Concours standard. Includes our products for surface care, leather seats, wood, plastics, vinyl, wheels, tyres, chrome, brass, nickel, glass. Price: add **£300.00** to your wax selection (see above)

Swissvax «Entry Collection»
The perfect introduction for your first 10 Swissvax applications. And it comes in its own handy cooler bag. You will cause a sensation when you use these hand-made products for the first time. Price: add **£85.00** to your wax selection (see above)

Swissvax Leather Care Kit
Easy to use and everything you need to clean and maintain your leather in perfect condition. With UV-protection.
Price: **£55.00**

More information? Ask for our famous 60-page Swissvax Handbook on car care. It's free!

SWISSVAX INTERNATIONAL

AUSTRALIA · AUSTRIA · BELGIUM · BRUNEI · CYPRUS · FINLAND · FRANCE · GERMANY · HONG KONG · INDONESIA · ITALY · JAPAN · KOREA · MALAYSIA · MALTA · MONACO · NETHERLANDS
NORWAY · PHILIPPINES · POLAND · ROMANIA · SINGAPORE · SOUTH AFRICA · SPAIN · SWITZERLAND · TAIWAN · THAILAND · UNITED KINGDOM · USA

SWISSVAX AG · CH-8117 FÄLLANDEN · TEL. +41(0)840 850 850 · FAX +41(0)44 730 45 02 · SALES@SWISSVAX.COM · WWW.SWISSVAX.COM

SWISSVAX UNITED KINGDOM

SWISSVAX UK · UNIT 14 · NIDD VALLEY BUSINESS PARK · KNARESBOROUGH HG5 9JA · PHONE 0870 240 7520 · SALES@SWISSVAX.CO.UK · WWW.SWISSVAX.CO.UK

CLASSICS IN CAMERA

Lamborghini Jota
MARK DIXON

Actually, it's a replica of the 1970 one-off Jota prototype, commissioned by Miura fan Piet Pulford and built from a tired early Miura donor car. *Octane* deputy editor Mark Dixon snapped this co-driver's view during the 2006 Miura 40th Anniversary Tour.

CLASSICS IN CAMERA 27

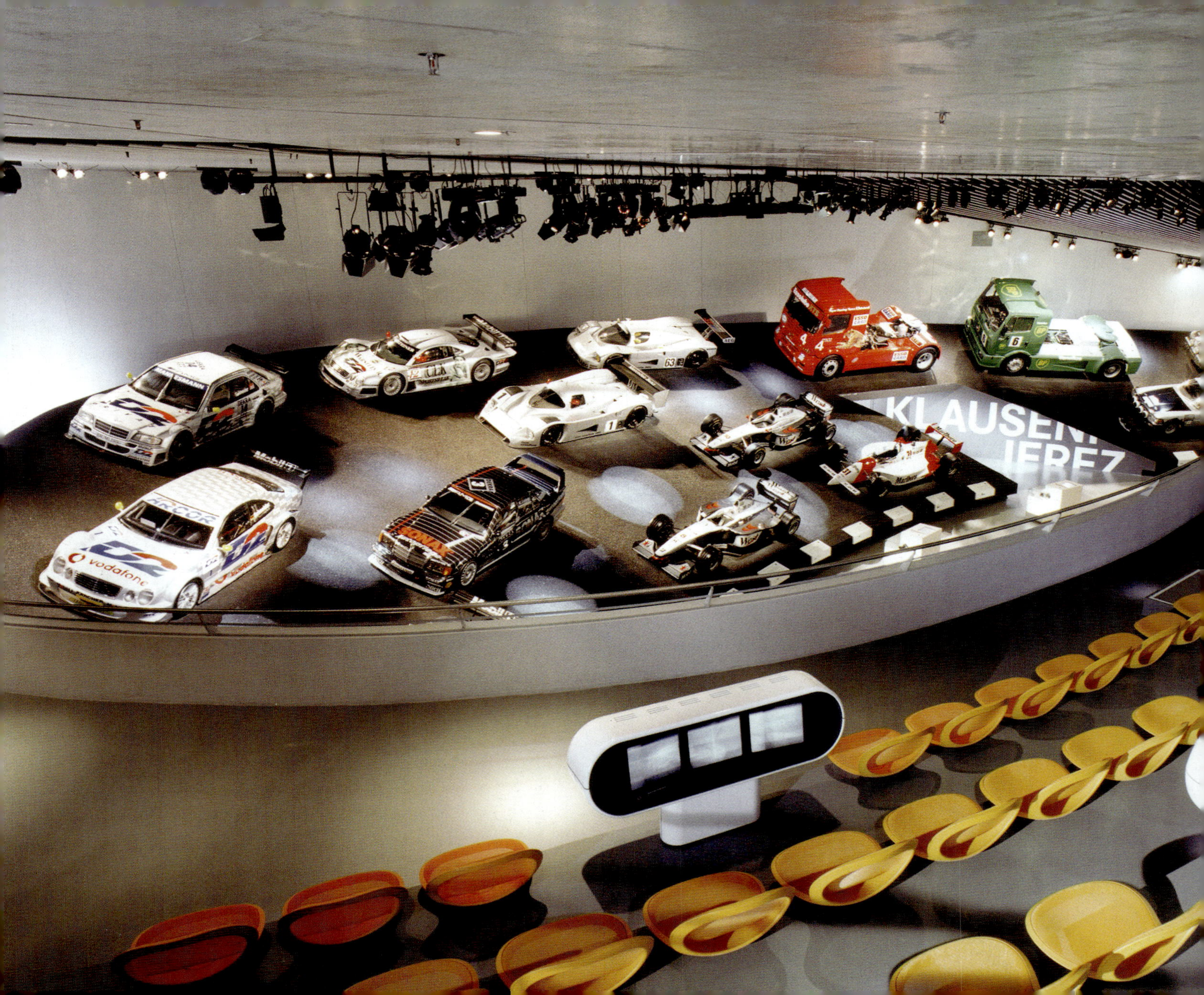
vodafone

Mercedes-Benz museum

In 2006 Mercedes opened a brand-new museum in a stunning building that dominates the Stuttgart skyline. The figures are impressive: nine levels, 160 vehicles, 1500 other exhibits – and a 5km walk if you're determined to see everything in the double-helix-inspired structure.

CLASSICS IN CAMERA

Mille Miglia
MARK DIXON

No event in the world can compare with Italy's Mille Miglia, which, as *Octane* editor Robert Coucher wrote after his drive in 2007, 'rolls Political Correctness up into one giant spliff and sets fire to it'.

Lamborghini Gallardo
MARK DIXON

Would you like to get a 520bhp Lambo' sideways on snow and ice? That's what Lamborghini encouraged at its Winter Driving Academy, intended to improve owners' car control *in extremis*.

Richard Petty – and girls
PETER ROBAIN

The Goodwood Festival of Speed has a tradition of attracting famous drivers past and present: in 2006 they included seven-times NASCAR champ Richard Petty and his 1972 Dodge Charger. The girls are younger than either, but Petty doesn't appear to be complaining...

CLASSICS IN CAMERA 33

Jaguar XJ220
JOHN COLLEY

Shunned by supercar enthusiasts for years after its promised V12 was superseded in production by a twin-turbo V6, Jaguar's supercar has now found a new generation of fans, encouraged by UK specialist Don Law Racing which has sorted many of the original's failings.

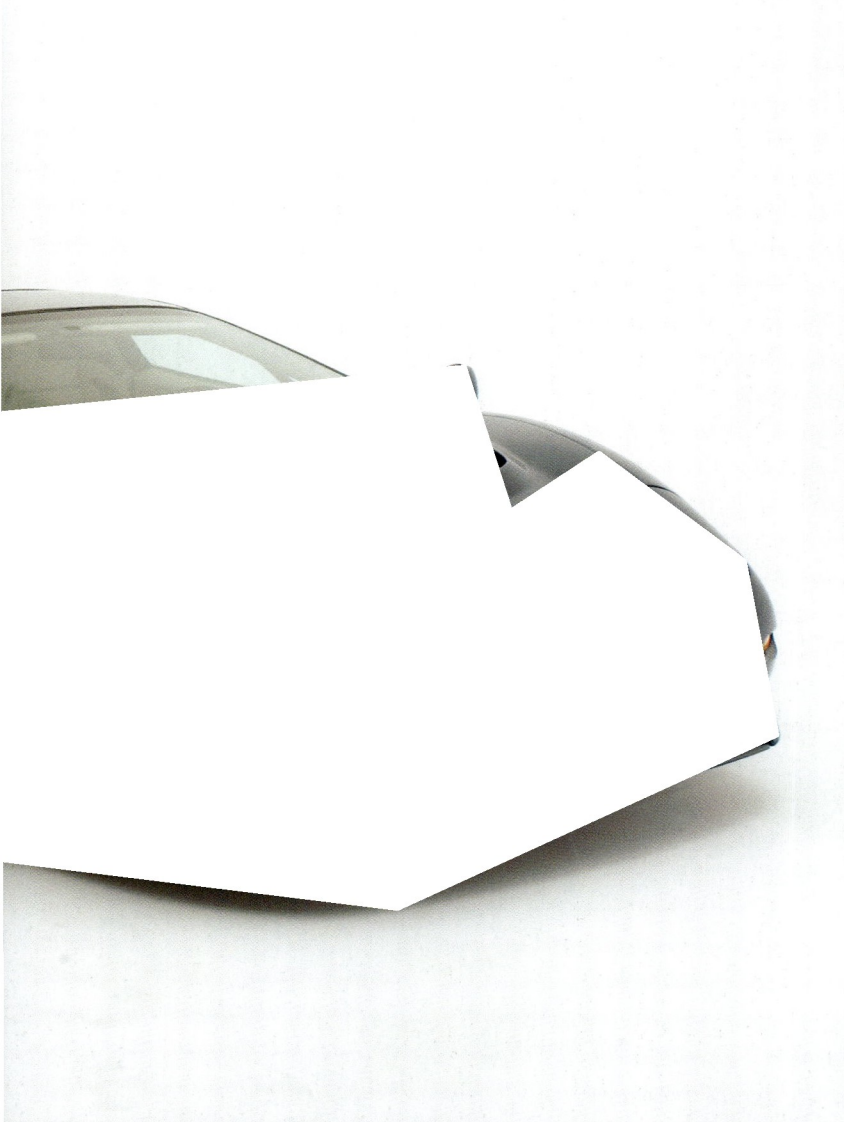

Hot Rod Hayride
MATTHEW HOWELL

It's not just cars, it's a way of life…
The UK's biggest gathering of period-style hot rods, the Hot Rod Hayride, is a 1950s-style celebration of an alternative culture, where people aren't afraid to get down and dirty.

1907 Renault
PAUL HARMER
A Renault very much like this won
the first-ever Grand Prix, held in
France in 1906. The main difference
is that this 1907 model has an
engine of only 7.5 litres capacity;
the 1906 GP car's was 12.8 litres.

tries to get its nose into the picture.

Lounge Chair & Ottoman
Design: Charles & Ray Eames, 1956

Designed to last for generations.
Since 1956 the Eames Lounge Chair has been
the modern icon of luxury and comfort.

vitra.
The Authorised Original

Experience the Lounge Chair at the following Vitra retailers: **Belfast** Living Space 7-15 Oxford Street BT1 3LA 02890 244 333 **Brighton** The Lollipop Shoppe Trafalgar Street BN1 4ED 01273 699 119 **Liverpool** Utility60 Bold Street L1 4EA 0151 708 4192 **London** The Aram Store 110 Drury Lane WC2B 5SG 020 7557 7557, Chaplins 477-507 Uxbridge Road HA5 4JS 020 8421 1779, The Conran Shop 81 Fulham Road SW3 6RD 020 7589 7401, Couch Potato Company 23 Hampton Road TW2 5QE 020 8894 1333, Geoffrey Drayton 85 Hampstead Road NW1 2PL 020 7387 5840, Skandium 86 Marylebone High Street W1U 4QS 020 7935 2077, TwentyTwentyOne 18C River Street N1 2UA 020 7837 1900, Workspirit 37 Bermondsey Wall West SE16 4RN **Manchester** Urbansuite 2 New George Street M4 4AE 0161 831 9966, **Sheffield** Electric Works Sheffield Digital Campus S1 2BJ 0845 456 2200, **Wakefield** Yorkshire Sculpture Park West Bretton WF4 4LG 01924 832 631 www.vitra.com

Vitra is the only authorised manufacturer of all Eames furniture designs for Europe and the Middle East. Historic Eames Family photos © Eames Office LLC.
Lounge Chair & Ottoman: © Vitra ®

CLASSICS IN CAMERA

Ferrari 250GTO

An unusual viewpoint for this sequence of photos charting the restoration of GTO no. 3527GT by UK specialist Mototechnique. Nearly 2500 hours were spent reworking a car that had been heavily raced (and crashed) since it was originally built in 1962.

Villa d'Este Concours
MARTYN GODDARD

Held on the shores of Lake Como, Villa d'Este is Europe's classiest concours. The car is Pininfarina's Ferrari 206 prototype; the ankles belong to the daughter of a prominent Italian car collector…

Nile Trial
GERARD BROWN

Motoring as it used to be on the Endurance Rally Association's 15-day adventure in North Africa, which travelled through Tunisia, Libya – the first time anyone had rallied through here – and Egypt.

Bentley 8 Litre
LAT / RICHARD C MOSS
Billed as 'motoring in its finest form' by *The Autocar*, the ultimate Bentley was one of the most expensive cars of the vintage period. The era's own 'credit crunch' killed it off: production stopped when Rolls-Royce took over the failed marque in 1931.

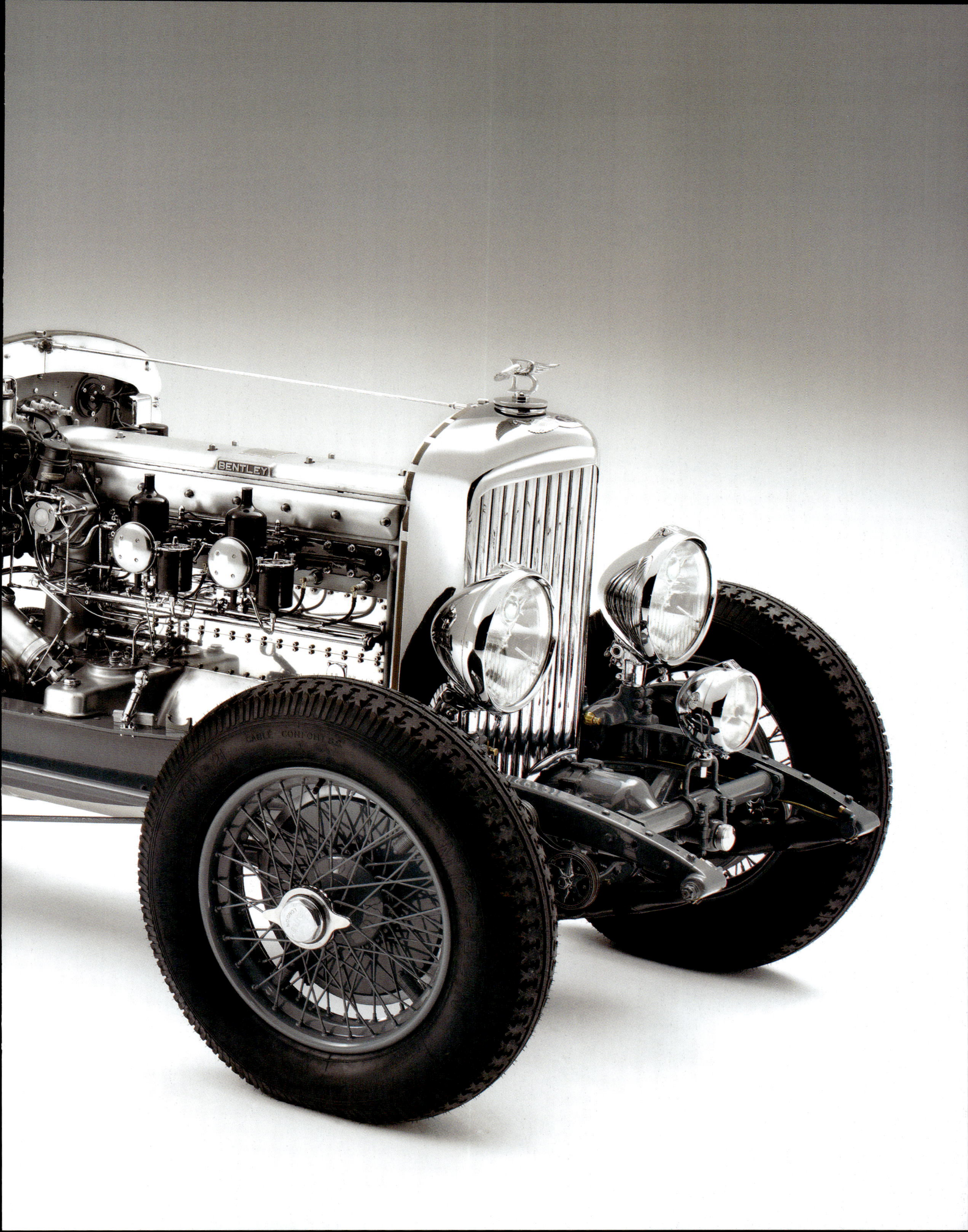
BENTLEY

CLASSICS IN CAMERA

DeLorean DMC-12
GEORGE BAMFORD

Its stainless steel body panels and gullwing doors gave the DeLorean true supercar looks, even if its 2.7-litre V6 couldn't quite deliver – but the *Back to the Future* films and John Z DeLorean's own chequered history (he was caught in an FBI drugs sting) have ensured its fame.

~ Sales ~ Service ~ Coachwork ~ Parts ~ Transport ~

A Snap Shot of RR&B Garages
one of the leading Independent Rolls-Royce & Bentley Motor Car Specialists...

Sales

We only offer the finest examples of Rolls-Royce and Bentley models ranging from the Rolls-Royce Silver Ghost and Vintage Bentley 3 litre through to the latest Rolls-Royce Phantom and Bentley Arnage. Please take the time to visit our website for details of cars currently available. If you cannot find the car with the specification you require, we will be pleased to source the right model for you. We sell many cars without marketing them so welcome your enquiry.

Service & Mechanical Overhaul

We have highly skilled and experienced technicians for all the models, who are dedicated and have a passion for the Marques. To assist them, our workshops have specialist equipment to deal with the intricacy of the vintage cars through to the advanced electronics of the current models. Whether you have requirements for a full chassis and engine restoration, a scheduled service or the replacement of a light bulb, our technicians will be pleased to assist.

Coachwork & Restoration

Our skilled craftsmen have an eye for the finest of detail, from the rectification of a minor scratch using the latest and correct paint technology, insurance approved accident repairs - returning the cars to an unmarked condition, or a ground up restoration to concours standards including interior trim, wood facia refinishing and bespoke upgrades.

Parts & Accessories

We have a significant stock holding of genuine Rolls-Royce & Bentley parts not only the routine service components but some major components too. Our membership of the Rolls-Royce & Bentley Specialist Association gives us access to many more high quality remanufactured parts that would otherwise be obsolete. Our parts service also distribute parts to owners and other garages worldwide.

Transport

We have our own specialist covered transporter to assist clients within the UK to collect & deliver their prize vehicles. For our overseas clients we are pleased to arrange collection and delivery through a network of specialist transport companies.

RR&B Garages Limited Forbes House, Harris Business Park, Hanbury Road, Stoke Prior, Bromsgrove, Worcs. B60 4BD
Tel: +44 (0)1527 876513   Fax: +44 (0)1527 877229
Email: sales@rrb-garages.com   www.rrb-garages.com

RR&B
GARAGES

MGB race & rally cars
PAUL HARMER

Its mantle as the sports car for everyman has now been taken over by the Mazda MX-5 but, ironically, the MGB has found a new respect among enthusiasts for its potential as a serious competition car.

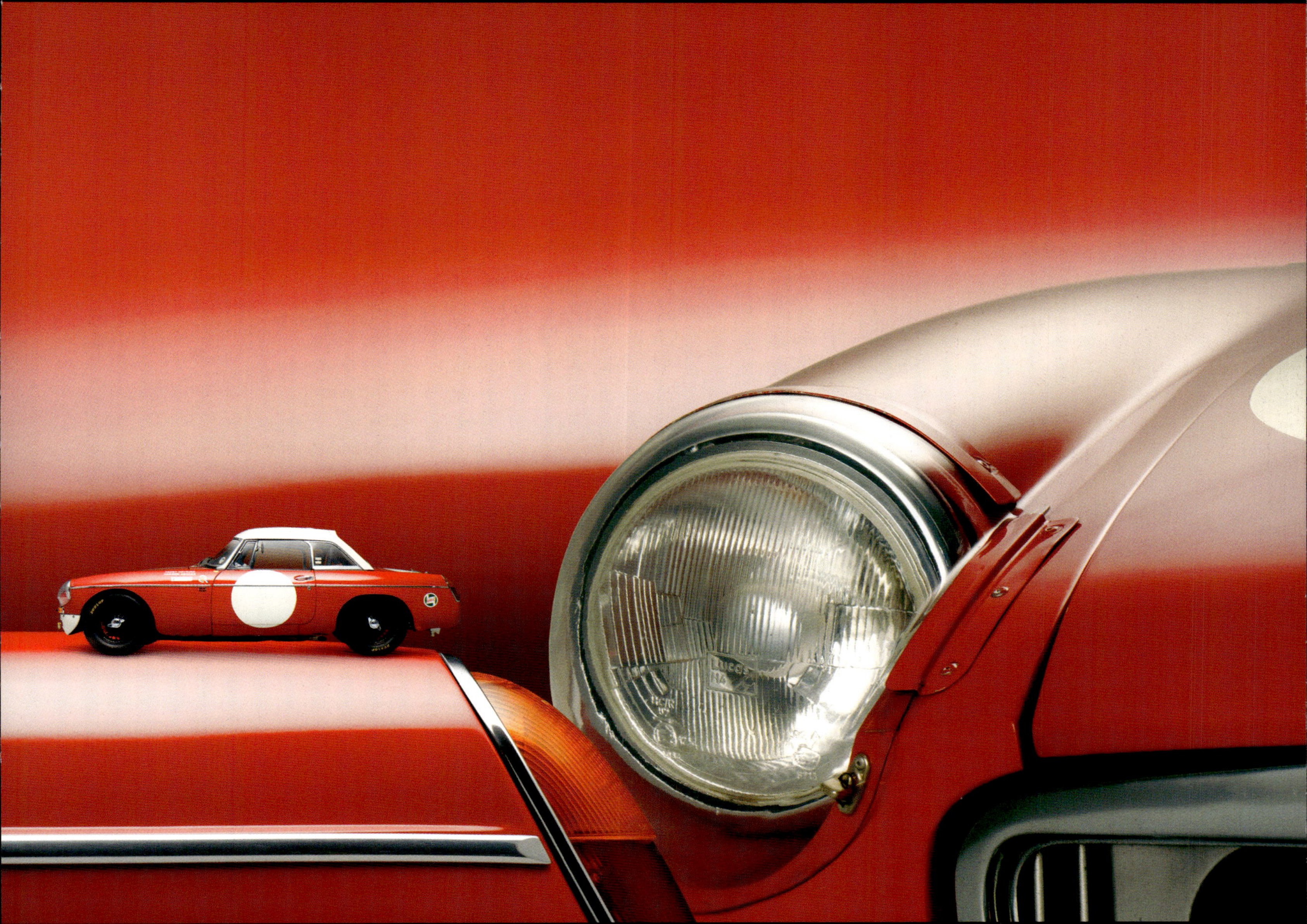

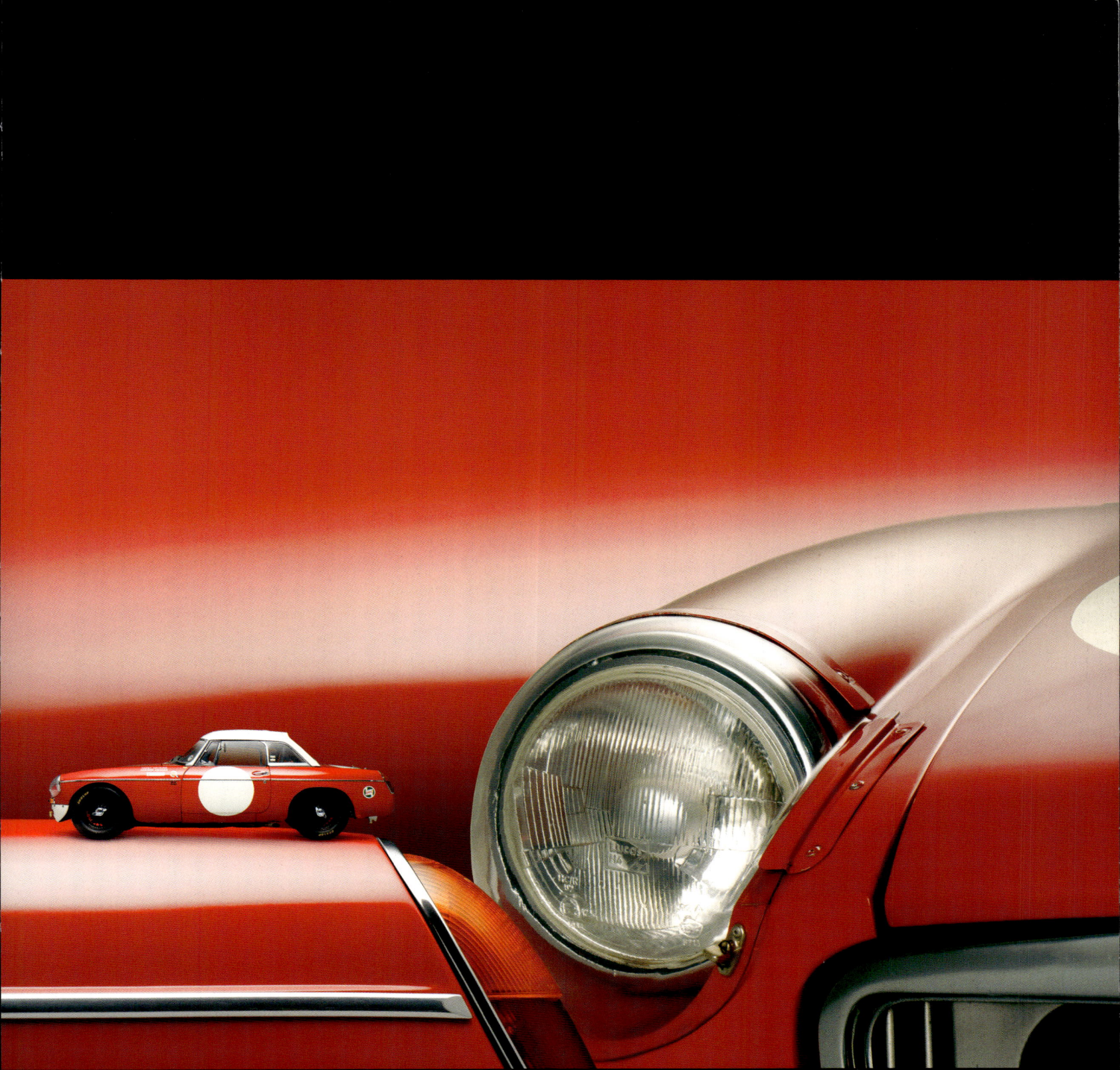

CLASSICS IN CAMERA

Bugatti in the lake
Divers from a Swiss scuba club (www.subascona.com) salvage a Type 22 which spent more than 70 years lying at the bottom of Lake Maggiore, after being dumped to avoid import duties.

CLASSIC CARS

Paul Hudson

paul.hudson@telegraph.co.uk @paul_hudson_dt

HIDDEN VALUE

A barn-find of 60 rare cars in France is expected to fetch up to £12m at auction next year

A picture tells a thousand words, apparently, but the images on this page can only hint at the importance of a barn-find collection in deepest France, containing about 60 rare cars worth an estimated €12-15million (£9.4-£11.8million), that had lain undisturbed for almost 40 years.

Discovered only three months ago, the collection is being sold at the Artcurial sale in Paris on February 6 during the annual Retromobile classic car show and represents perhaps the last opportunity for collectors to acquire and restore some of the finest cars from the Thirties, Forties and Fifties.

Not only is it a historically important collection of the French coachbuilder's art, with examples from Chapron, Saoutchik and Million-Guiet, there's also the small matter of a Ferrari California SWB discovered semi-submerged under bundles of old magazines. The picture on the right shows precisely

THIS WEEK ON THE TELEGRAPH CARS YOUTUBE CHANNEL

Visit our YouTube channel for video reviews of the latest cars on sale, presented by Rebecca Jackson and Chris Knapman. They are all free to watch, and if you subscribe we'll notify you each week when a new one is uploaded – the perfect start to choosing your next new car. Videos can be found by visiting **tgr.ph/1yxW1P4**

MERCEDES GLA 45 AMG
This is a crossover with the power to match a sports car. Rebecca Jackson gets behind the wheel of the GLA for performance fans.

Watch the video at:
tgr.ph/1FLFUxm

AUDI TT
The TT is one of the most popular sports cars on sale, and with its trendy interior, the latest version is going to be another hit.

Watch the video at:
tgr.ph/1SO3MDW

LEXUS NX300h
The Lexus NX is an SUV with low running costs and sharp styling, but can it cut it against rivals such as the BMW X3?

Watch the video at:
tgr.ph/12rqf8r

THE FACTS

SUZUKI VITARA

TESTED
1,586cc four-cylinder petrol, five-speed manual gearbox, four-wheel drive (two-wheel drive an option)

PRICE/ON SALE
£14,000-£19,500 (est)/spring 2015

POWER/TORQUE
118bhp @ 6,000rpm / 115lb ft @ 4,400rpm

TOP SPEED
115mph (est)

ACCELERATION
0-62mph in 9.5sec (est)

FUEL ECONOMY
43.5mpg/50.4mpg (EU Urban/Combined). On test 32mpg

CO$_2$ EMISSIONS
130g/km

VED BAND
D (£0 first year, £110 thereafter)

VERDICT
Rework of an old theme shows what can be done with some ordinary parts and attention to detail. But some of its controls feel slapdash, and with four-wheel drive and a diesel engine it's quite expensive

RATING
★★★☆☆

Sophistication: the Vitara drives well and comes well equipped

Peter Stevens
MARK DIXON

Car designer Peter Stevens – who is best known for the McLaren F1 road car – has a passion for hot rods, and a studio filled with interesting mementoes of a long career.

CLASSICS IN CAMERA

Honda NSX
MATTHEW HOWELL

The bright lights and broad pavements of after-hours Milton Keynes were perfect for this long-exposure shot of Honda (UK)'s own NSX – the car in which Ayrton Senna was reputedly stopped for speeding while over here for the British Grand Prix.

CLASSICS IN CAMERA

Aston Martin 'A3'
MATTHEW HOWELL

The oldest surviving Aston in the world, chassis number three was built in 1921 and recently restored for the Aston Martin Heritage Trust. Its light weight makes it nippy on the road, despite having only a 1389cc sidevalve engine.

CLASSICS IN CAMERA

Aston Martin Vanquish
GEORGE BAMFORD
Not just any Vanquish, however, but one from the Bond film *Die Another Day*. At the time, Aston Martin and Jaguar were owned by Ford, so the villain's car was a Jaguar XKR. Bond and the Aston won, not surprisingly.

Lotus Esprit S1
GEORGE BAMFORD
Another Bond car, this time from *The Spy Who Loved Me*, in which it memorably transformed into a submarine. Roger Moore and Barbara Bach struggled to compete as the co-stars...

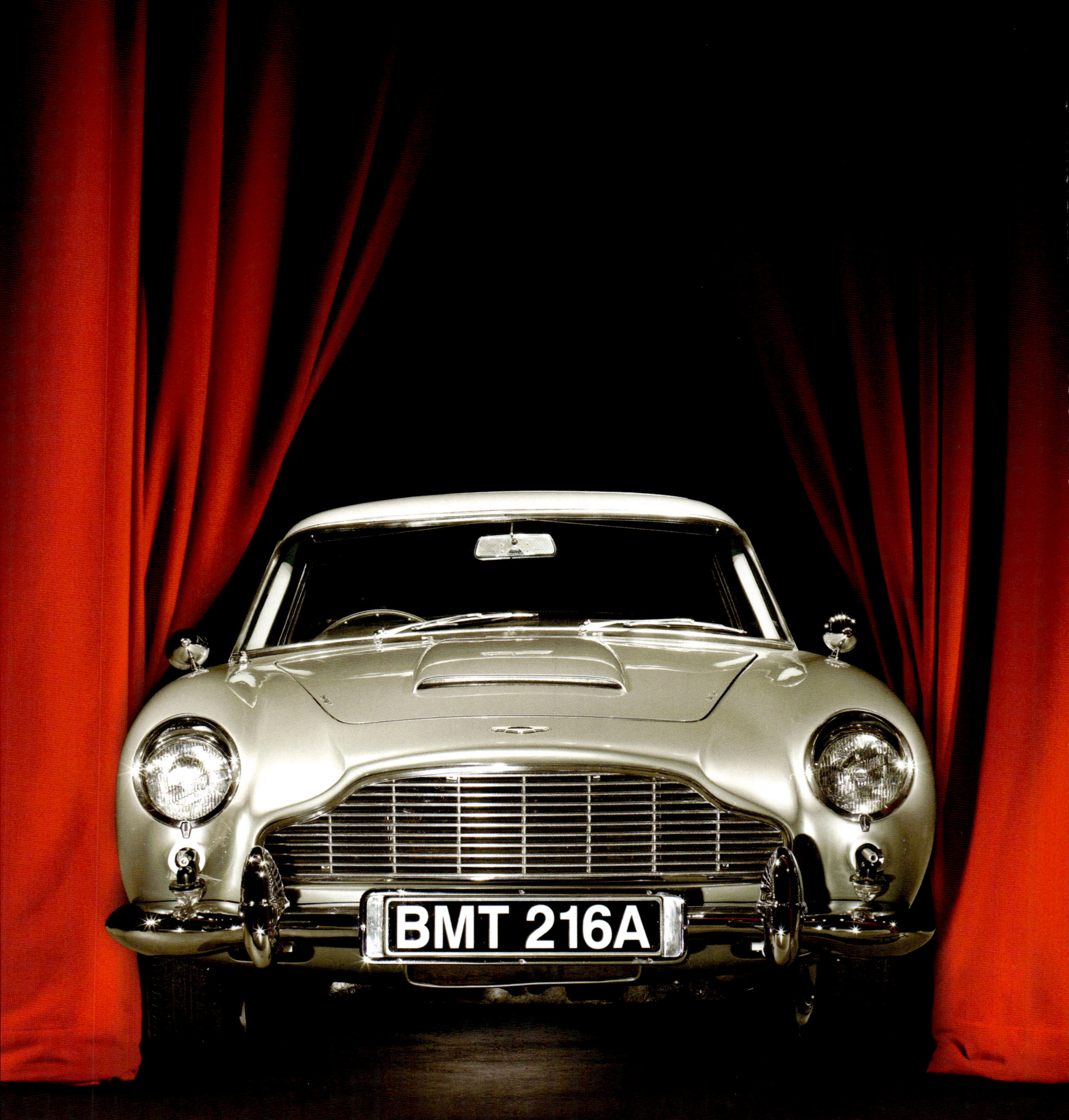
BMT 216A

Aston Martin DB5
GEORGE BAMFORD
'Without doubt the most famous Bond car ever, the DB5 appeared in both *Goldfinger* and *Thunderball*. Four cars were converted to Bond spec for filming and publicity tours; only two made it on screen, and this is the sole survivor of the pair.

CLASSICS IN CAMERA

Porsche 917 & Ferrari 512S
PAUL HARMER

The ultimate sports racers of their era, these deadly rivals packed 500+bhp engines into shells weighing about 800kg – and both could top 200mph.

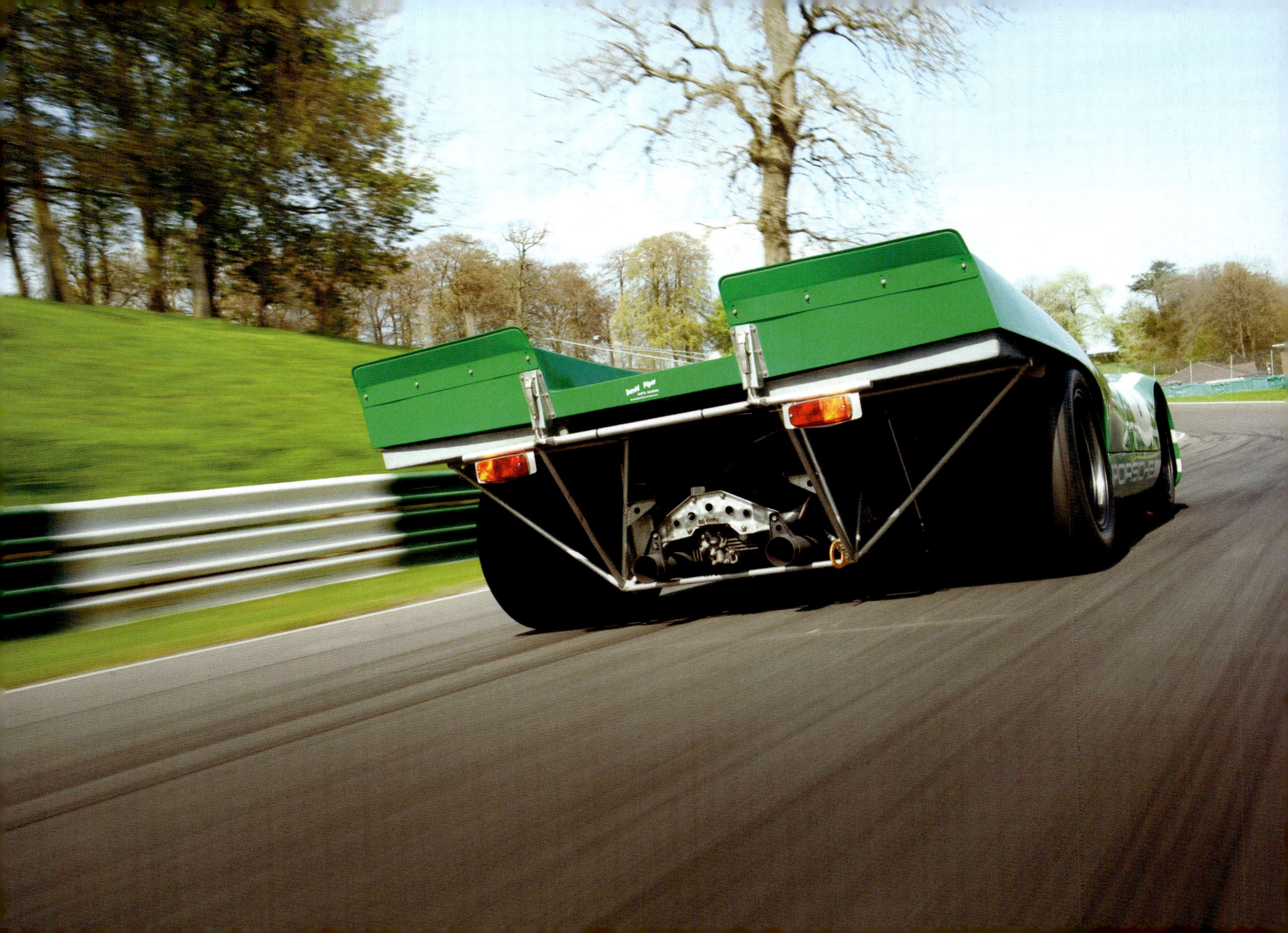

CLASSICS IN CAMERA

Zagato
MARK DIXON

Italian design house Zagato was
founded in 1919 and is headed
by Andrea Zagato (pictured

CLASSICS IN CAMERA

Bentley racing cars
PAUL HARMER

To publicise the Bentley Drivers Club's 60th anniversary races at Silverstone, members brought a diverse selection of models along for an *Octane* track test. All these cars are raced regularly –including that unlikely-looking Turbo R saloon!

CLASSICS IN CAMERA

Ford Baja Bronco
MARK DIXON
Believe it or not, this limited-edition 4x4, an early-'70s tribute to the Parnelli Jones rally car, is usually kept in concours condition. A photoshoot in a quarry soon changed that…

Bugatti 'Black Bess'
TIM ANDREW

'Black Bess', a 1913 5-litre Bugatti, is a proper Edwardian supercar and one of the most desirable of all Bugattis. She was sold at auction in early 2009 for almost 2.5 million euros.

CLASSICS IN CAMERA

Porsche 356s
PAUL HARMER

The same, but different – this assembly of Porsche's iconic 356 model includes, clockwise from foreground, a silver 1953 'Pre-A' Coupé, red 1963 Carrera 2 GT Coupé, silver 1959 Convertible D and a last-of-the-line white SC Cabriolet.

CLASSICS IN CAMERA

CLASSICS IN CAMERA

Lamborghini Countach
MATTHEW HOWELL

Criticised when new for being big and unwieldy, the Countach LP400 now looks relatively small – such is progress. It's still the dream car for many grown men who were children when it appeared in the early '70s.

CLASSICS IN CAMERA 71

CLASSICS IN CAMERA

Silver Arrows
MARK DIXON

One of the first-ever meetings of the legendary Mercedes-Benz and Auto Union Silver Arrows was at the daunting Klausenpass mountain climb near Linthal in the Swiss Alps. Over 70 years on, they were reunited exclusively once again, for *Octane* magazine.

Morgan Plus Four
PAUL HARMER

Believe it or not, this old-fashioned-looking Morgan took 1st in the 2-litre GT class at Le Mans in 1962. Its owner, Chris Lawrence, bought it for £600 from a used-car lot and used his engine-tuning prowess to turn it into a Porsche 356-beater.

ONE HUNDRED YEARS OF A DRIVING PASSION

To see for yourself what makes a Morgan so special, contact your nearest dealer to arrange a test drive.
For more information visit morgan-motor.co.uk

Melvyn Rutter Ltd
Hertfordshire
01279 725 725
www.melvyn-rutter.co.uk

Newtown Motors
Wales
01633 485 251
info@newtown-motors.co.uk

Richard Thorne Classic Cars
Berkshire
0118 9831200
www.rtcc.co.uk

John Gill Ltd
Yorkshire
01677 423134
carolgill@johngill.co.uk

Berrybrook Motors Ltd
Devon
01392 833 301
www.berrybrook.co.uk

Lifes Motors Ltd
Lancashire
01704 531 375
sales@lifesmotors.com

Stratton Motor Company
Norfolk
01508 530 491
www.strattonmotorcompany.com

Perranwell Garage
Cornwall
01872 863 037
alan@perranwell.co.uk

Mike Duncan
Worcestershire
01299 250 025
www.morgans4sale.co.uk

Williams Morgan
Bristol
0800 0582983
www.williamsautomobiles.com

Ledgerwood Morgan
Lincolnshire
01724 733228
phil@philledgerwoodwanadoo.co.uk

Mole Valley
Surrey
01306 710088
www.mole-valley.co.uk

Brands Hatch Morgan Ltd
Kent
01732 882 017
sales@morgan-cars.com

I & J Macdonald Ltd
Durham
01207 520 916
info@macdonald-racing.com

Morgan Motor Company
Worcestershire
01684 573104
adrian.jones@morgan-motor.co.uk

Russell Paterson Morgan
Scotland
01738 44 4004
russell@rpm-morgan.co.uk

SGT
Berkshire
01628 605 353
www.sgt.co.uk

Car shown Roadster 3.0 V6 - own it from £38,400
Morgan range from £27,250 ex factory on the road
Official Fuel consumption in mpg (litres/100km) for the Morgan range
Urban 17.3 (16.3) - 34.0 (8.3) Extra Urban 34.8 (8.1) - 57.6 (4.9)
Combined 25.4 (11.1) - 45.5 (6.2) CO_2 emissions 269 - 139.7 g/km

Allon White Sports Cars
Bedfordshire
0845 3457666
www.allonwhite.co.uk

MORGAN
DRIVEN AT HEART

CLASSICS IN CAMERA

**Aston Martin
DB4 & DB5**
MICHAEL BAILIE

Given the choice of this pairing,
most would probably opt for
the Silver Birch DB5 – as driven
by a certain secret agent. But
the green DB4 Series I has a
delicacy that sets it apart as one
of the most elegant '50s designs.

CLASSICS IN CAMERA

CLASSICS IN CAMERA

Alfa Romeo 8C 2300

One of the greatest, perhaps *the* greatest, of pre-war sports cars, the 8C 2300 notched up a formidable competition record. That was largely due to its superb eight-cylinder, double-overhead-cam engine, designed by Alfa engineer Vittorio Jano.

CLASSICS IN CAMERA

CLASSICS IN CAMERA

Bugatti EB110
MARK DIXON

Ettore Bugatti's villa at Molsheim, whose grounds now house the Veyron plant, abuts onto a wonderful tree-lined road: the perfect 1920s setting for this 1990s supercar.

Peter Ratcliffe

LEGENDS IN TIME
THE COLLECTION THE DRIVERS SIGN

THE MOSS SIGNED COLLECTION

Signed by Stirling Moss with photo

Signed by Stirling Moss with photo

Signed by Stirling Moss with photo

Signed by Juan Manuel Fangio and Stirling Moss with photos

Signed by Stirling Moss with photo

Portrait signed by Stirling Moss with photo

Signed by Stirling Moss with photo

Established 1988

Tel: (44) 01344 872911

www.legendsintime.co.uk

CLASSICS IN CAMERA

Lamborghini Murciélago & Ferrari 599GTB
MATTHEW HOWELL

The latest versions of Italy's supercar champs – the Murciélago 670-4 SV and 599GTB with HGTE handling package – exhibit the differences in style and character that have always set these two rival marques apart. You'd kill to own either, of course…

CLASSICS IN CAMERA 83

CLASSICS IN CAMERA

Jaguar XKSS
JASON FURNARI
Jaguar's devastating factory fire in February 1957 meant only 16 of these gorgeous, hugely fast sports racers were built. Based on the Le Mans-winning D-type, they were aimed squarely at the US market – Steve McQueen

CLASSICS IN CAMERA

Jaguar Mk2 3.4
MATTHEW HOWELL

In the heart of Brussels, classic car enthusiast Gilles Vink uses his fully restored 1960s Jaguar every day, having worked out that it's more cost-effective than leasing a BMW turbodiesel.

BEACHAM

IN PURSUIT OF PERFECTION

THE LATEST BEACHAM XK 150 V8 S
A NEW AGE OF CLASSICAL TOURING

In the history of motor vehicle manufacture only Beacham have taken 46 year old designs and redeveloped them with sympathetic synergy to the best of the old and the best of the new Jaguar motors and technology. Produced in very small numbers the Beacham E-Type, XK150 and MK2 V8 represent unique hand built works of motoring art under which cars with true heart, classic styling, performance and safety features combine to place them ahead of many modern high performance cars.

Beacham also restore to original factory specifications. Restorations are also offered for Aston Martin, Daimler, Rolls Royce and Bently.

For further information and ordering:
BEACHAM INDEPENDENT JAGUAR SPECIALISTS LTD. NEW ZEALAND
ph +64 274735432 | fax +64 6 878 8056 | greg@beacham-jaguar.co.nz | www.beacham-jaguar.co.nz

Lancia Stratos
PAUL HARMER

On its 1972 introduction, the first car purpose-built for Group 4 regs seemed more like a spaceship than a world rally contender. With its Ferrari engine and Bertone body, it soon became the machine other teams had to beat, from the heat of Africa to the snows of Scandinavia.

CLASSICS IN CAMERA 89

CLASSICS IN CAMERA

Peking-to-Paris Austin Seven
JOHN COLLEY

Eschewing the much-publicised Peking-Paris classic rally held in 2007, vintage car enthusiast Sebastian Welch did the same trip in his Austin Seven. He and co-driver Annabel Jones carried everything they needed in the car – with no support crew.

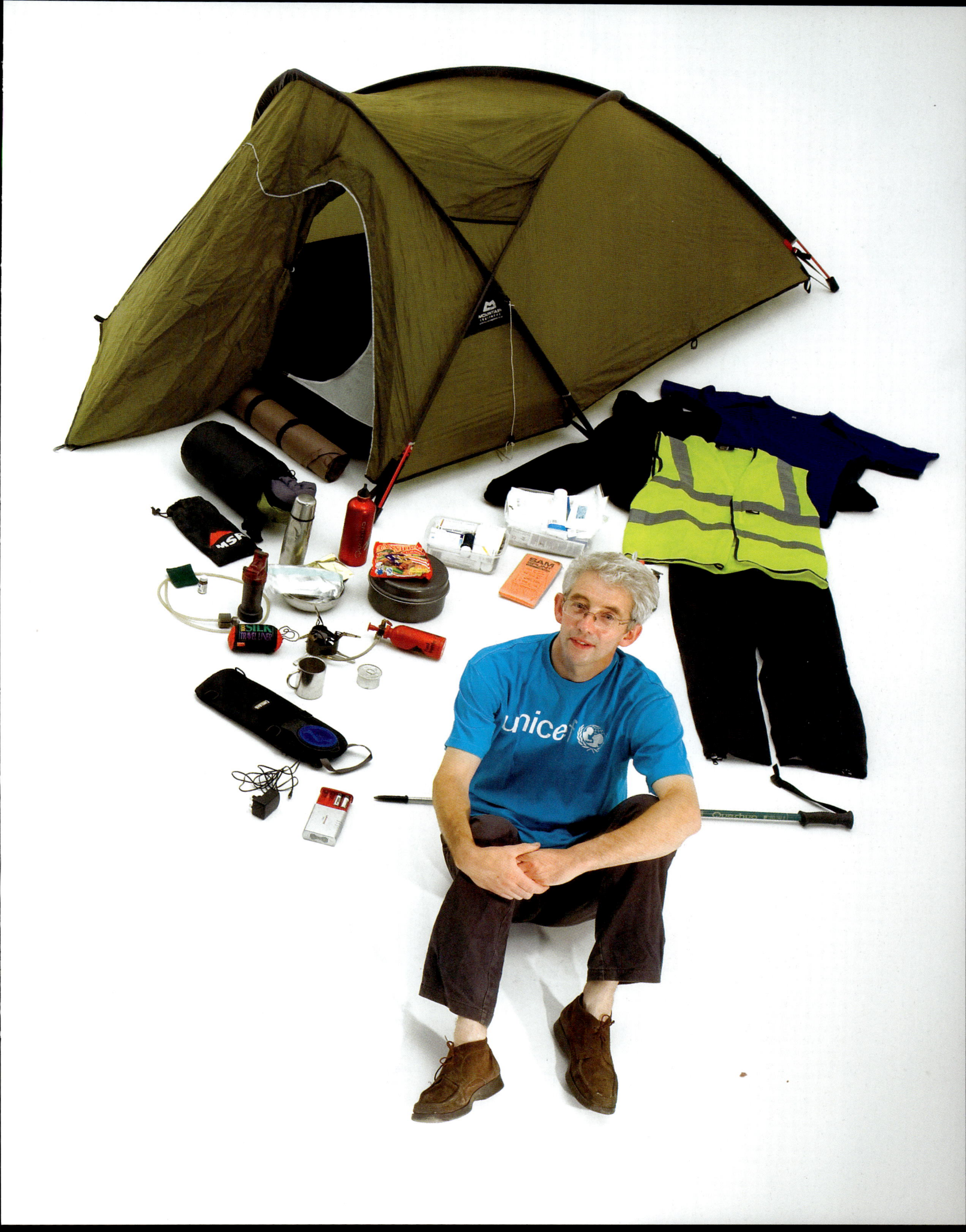
MSR
SILK
TRAVEL LINER
unicef

CLASSICS IN CAMERA

Aston at Le Mans
PAUL HARMER

Fighting 3am fatigue: the Lola-Aston Martin LMP1 car number 008 pits during its battle to become the first petrol-powered car home in its class at the 2009 Le Mans 24 Hours. It succeeded in its quest!

Blue Train Bentleys
DOMINIC FRASER
Daredevil Bentley Boy and marque chairman Captain Woolf Barnato beat famously rapid *Le Train Bleu* from

PADGETT MOTOR ENGINEERS
Rolls-Royce & Bentley Specialists
(1934 - 1965 models)

Fabrication and supply of the following services & parts:-

- Exhaust Systems
- Forged Pistons
- Valve gear
- Carburation & Porting
- Cast alloy brake drums
- Viscous crank dampers
- Carrillo Con-Rods
- Alloy Wheels
- Alloy Radiators
- Fine Limit Engine Balance
- Electronic Ignition
- Transmission upgrades.

Brooklands, Spanby, Sleaford. Lincolnshire. NG34 0BB

Email: jeremypadgett@btconnect.com Tel: 01529 240400 Fax: 01529 241041 Website: www.padgett-bentleyrestoration.co.uk

G&R CLASSICS
PASSION • DRIVING • PERFECTION

' The Greatest Cars require the finest paint and body refinishing

Call us now to discuss your project

www.gandrclassics.co.uk

Unit 3a , Spring Lane North, Malvern, WR 14 1BU. Tel: 01684 578808 — Mobile: 07802 575750 — Fax 01684 566966

CLASSICS IN CAMERA

BMW Z8
MARK DIXON

Apparently influenced by a 1960s Chevrolet Corvette, BMW's Z8 met a cool reception from the press when it appeared in the late-'90s, but is today cherished for its relaxed performance and subtly different style.

CLASSICS IN CAMERA

CLASSICS IN CAMERA

Bentley MkVI
MARK DIXON
Photographer Ivo Peters used his Bentley to chase his favourite subject, steam trains, in the 1950s and '60s. His car survives – as do a few of the engines he photographed.

Rolls-Royce Camargue
IAN DAWSON
At its 1975 launch this Pininfarina-bodied coupé was the world's most expensive production car: its £29,250 was twice the price of a Silver Shadow. It still turns heads today, even in car-jaded London.

CLASSICS IN CAMERA

Porsche 917 duo
MATTHEW HOWELL

Big Porsche is universally hailed as one of the greatest racing cars of our time, and veteran driver David Piper owns two – including Chassis 010, which he's contested since 1969.

CLASSICS IN CAMERA

Hornet special
MARK DIXON
Built on a chassis found in a
French hedge and powered by
a pair of 1920s Harley-Davidson
motorbike engines, this pre-war-
style Shelsley hillclimb special

Bugatti Atlantic, Veyron & EB110
MARK DIXON
Three generations of Bugatti
supercars, grouped around the
typically flamboyant staircase
outside Ettore Bugatti's old

Mercedes 380K

Far from being a bog-standard, if beautiful, example of the least fêted of the 1930s supercharged Mercedes, this one-off drophead features an experimental factory-fitted detachable hard-top.

CLASSICS IN CAMERA 105

1925 Chrysler 70 'Bluebird'
PAUL HARMER

A stunning recreation visits its spiritual home: Malcolm Campbell raced the original version of this car to victory at Brooklands on September 12, 1925, with a winning average speed of 99.61mph. He described his steed as 'Absolutely steady – most satisfactory!'

Rolls-Royce Phantom

Sumptuous saloon – only the second example to be exported to South Africa – meets supersonic cousin. The civilian-owned, ex-military English Electric Lightning interceptor boasts twin Rolls-Royce Avon engines giving a top speed of Mach 2.23 – and a climb rate of 50,000ft per minute.

CLASSICS IN CAMERA

Aston Martin DBR1
IAN DAWSON

No other Aston has achieved the motor sport success of this machine, and no other provokes the same appreciation from now-legendary drivers. *Octane* contributor and racer Mark Hales got behind the wheel in issue 3, in September 2003.

Aston Workshop

ASTON MARTIN SPECIALISTS   SALES | RESTORATION | PARTS | SERVICING

Photography by Tim Wallace www.ambientlife.co.uk

We are probably selling and restoring more Aston Martin's than any other Aston Martin specialist anywhere else in the world.
Why not register with our bespoke computerised database designed to obtain a new home for your vehicle or find you your dream Aston Martin at
www.aston.co.uk/crm_index/php/action/seller .
You can also subscribe to our NEW eNewsletter at http://www.aston.co.uk/mailinglist_index/php

www.aston.co.uk
www.astonart.com

Row Beamish Co Durham DH9 0RW Telephone +44 (0) 1207 233525 Fax +44 (0) 1207 232202 Email: astonworkshop@aston.co.uk

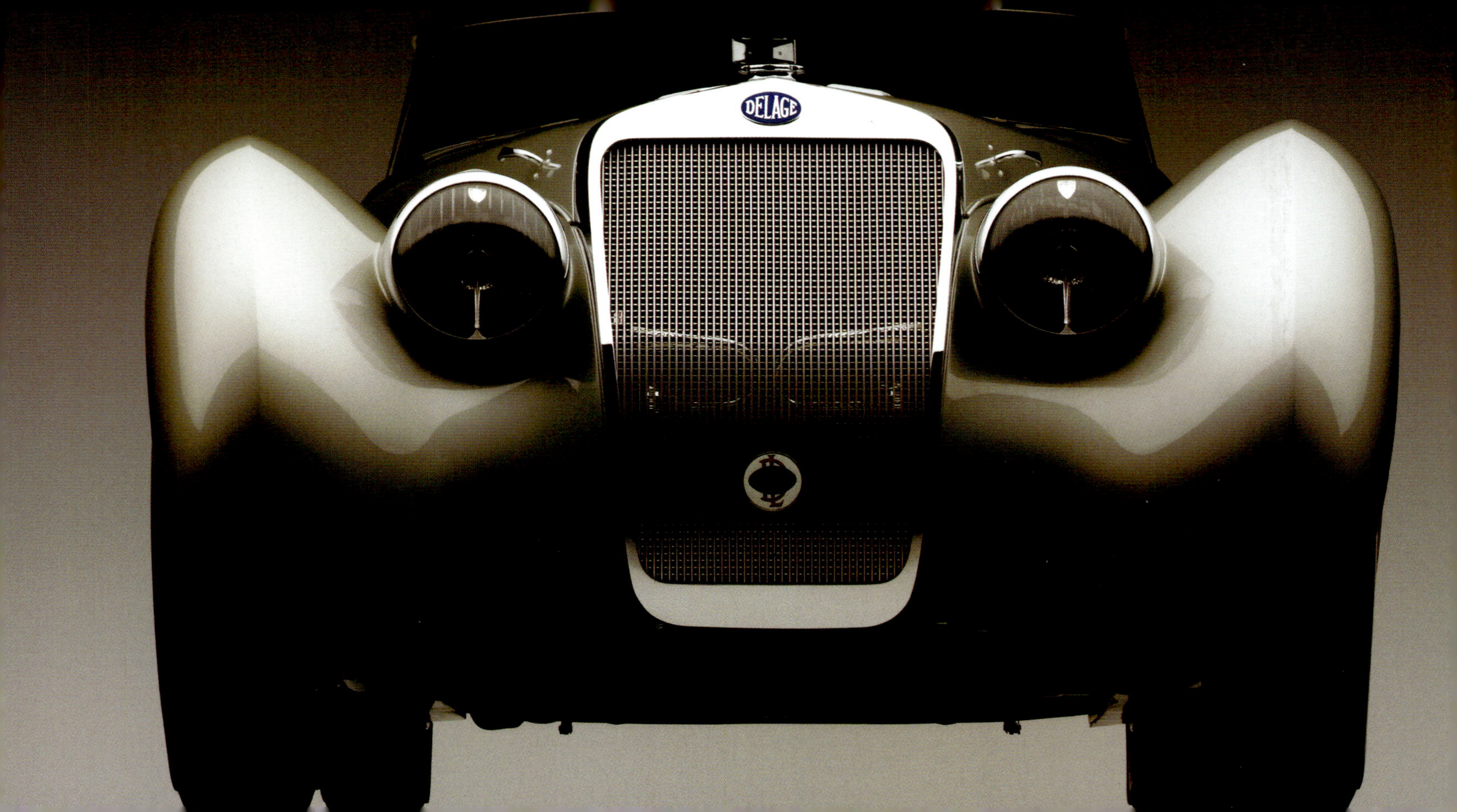
DELAGE

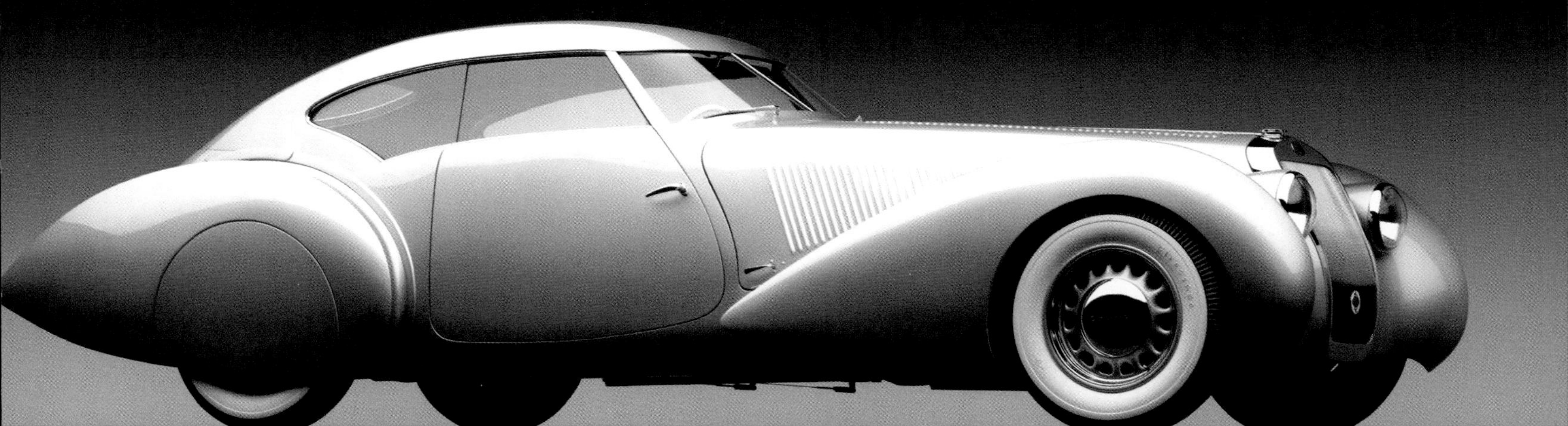

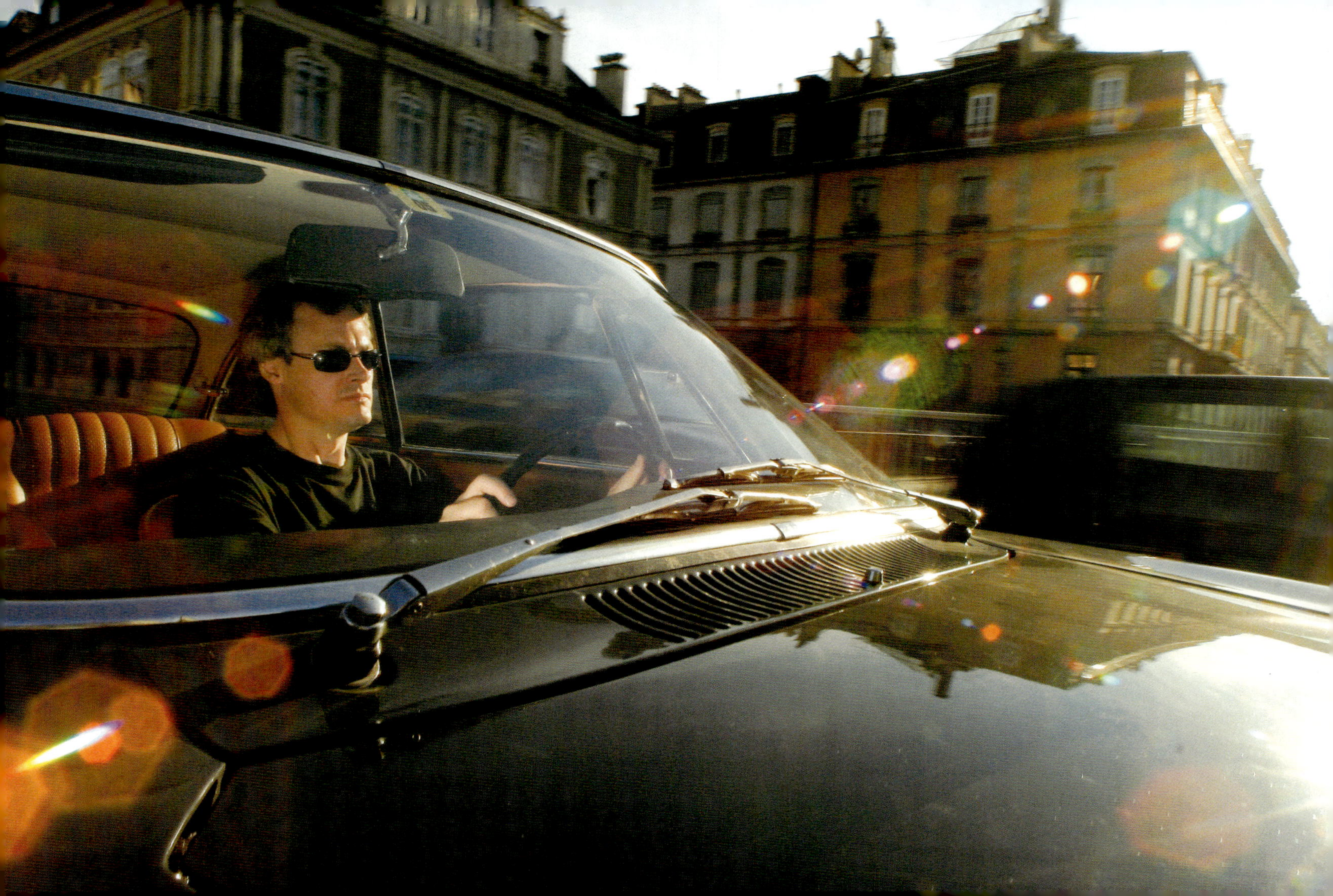

Alfa Romeo 1600GTV
IAN DAWSON

Octane deputy editor Mark Dixon drove this totally original Alfa coupé from London to Geneva for a feature. Goodwood's Lord March later bought the car for

CLASSICS IN CAMERA

Jay Leno
MARK DIXON

US chat show supremo Jay is a total, hands-on petrolhead. During an *Octane* visit to LA he took editor Robert Coucher for a ride in one of his favourite cars, a Stanley Steamer.

Itala 40hp
GERARD BROWN

In 1907, Prince Borghese's Itala won
the Peking-Paris rally. A century on,
British adventurers David and Karen
Ayre drove a sister car over the same

Paris-Dakar winner
MITSUBISHI

Thanks to its back-to-back rally victories, Mitsubishi's Pajero Evolution was the undisputed king of the desert in 2004 – and *Octane* headed to the dunes to experience the rally raid supremo first hand.

Ford GT
DANIEL BYRNE

Who said the 21st century 'retro' supercar wasn't suitable for long journeys? Motoring writer Jeremy Hart put the model's Gran Turismo moniker to the test by driving it 3000 miles across America.

Marathon men
MIKE JOHNSON
Thirty days, seven countries and 15,000km – it could only be the London to Sydney Marathon. Contenders strap in for airlift

Audi quattro
DAVID CORFIELD
With its 360bhp, 2143cc, five-cylinder engine and four-wheel-drive transmission, the quattro was an immediate Group B rally

CLASSICS IN CAMERA

Jaguar XK120, XK140 & XK150
MICHAEL BAILIE

This fabulous trio, brought together in the studio by Jaguar specialist JD Classics, represents the evolution of the XK series, from early, spatted 120 Roadster via luxurious 140 Drop Head Coupé to super-quick XK150 3.8S Fixed Head Coupé.

J.D Classics

Office: (01621) 879579 **Facsimile:** (01621) 850370 **Mobile:** (07850) 966005

THE FINEST SELECTION OF
XK JAGUARS

WE ARE THE PREMIER DEALER FOR CLASSIC JAGUARS. WE HAVE FULL SERVICING AND RESTORATION FACILITIES TO THE HIGHEST STANDARDS.

We urgently require for stock, more Classic Jaguars of the highest quality, particularly 'Genuine Competiton Cars' and XKs. If you own a superb Jaguar, and are thinking about selling, please contact us with an accurate description of your vehicle.

IF THE CAR YOU ARE LOOKING FOR IS NOT LISTED ABOVE, PLEASE TALK TO US ABOUT IT. WE ARE HAPPY TO DISCUSS EVERY ASPECT OF CLASSIC CAR OWNERSHIP INCLUDING CLASSIC CAR FINANCE, AND TO GIVE YOU OUR BEST ADVICE.

WEB SITE: www.jdclassics.co.uk
Email: jd@jdclassics.net
OFFICE: (01621) 879579 FACSIMILE: (01621) 850370
MOBILE NUMBER: (07850) 966005

J.D Classics

WYCKE HILL BUSINESS PARK, WYCKE HILL, MALDON, ESSEX CM9 6UZ, U.K.

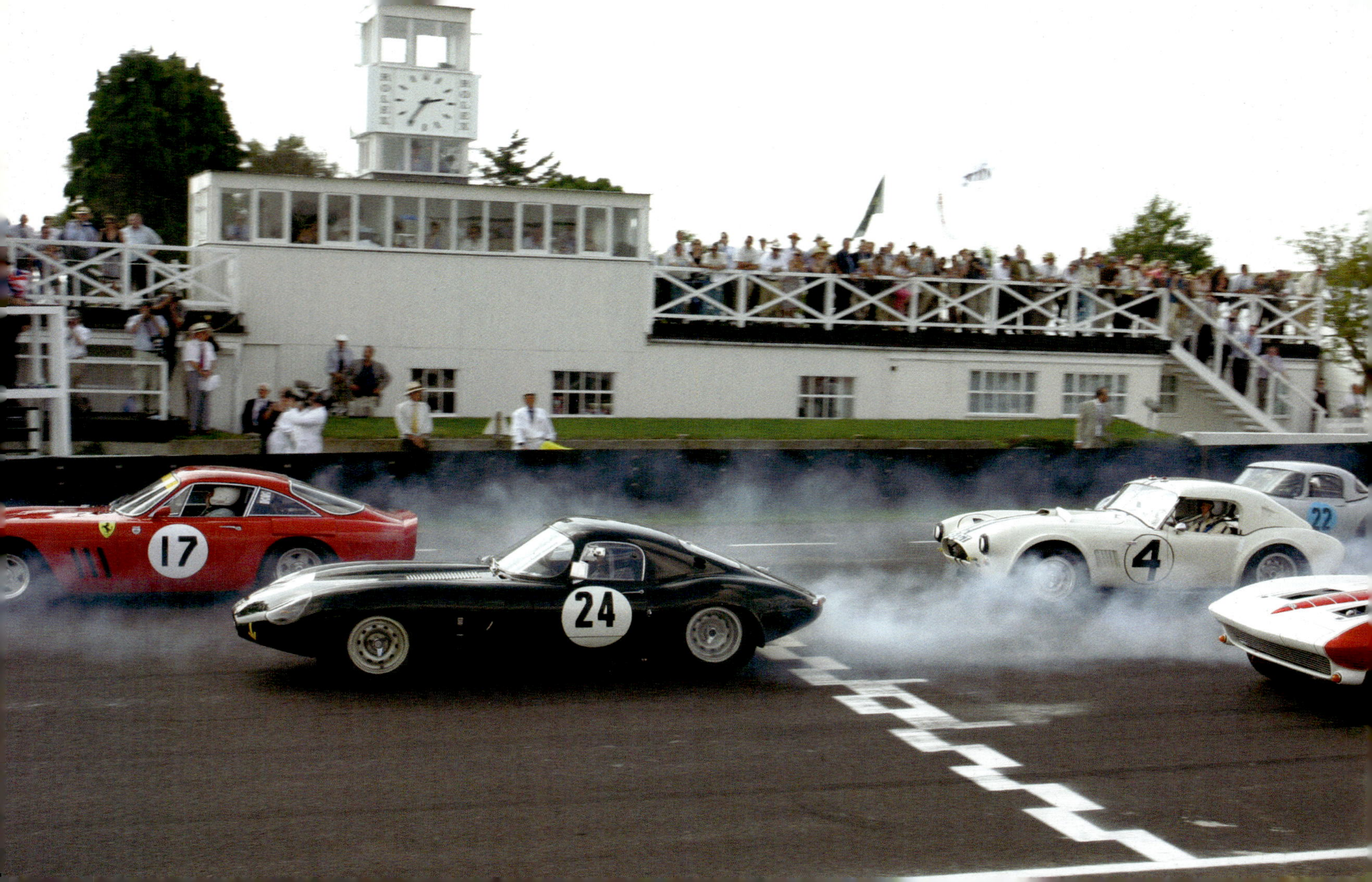
ROLEX
17
24
4
22

Goodwood Revival
STEVE HAVELOCK / JOHN COLLEY
Reliving the golden years of British motor sport, the world's greatest historic racing event takes place each September at Lord March's own West Sussex circuit. Period-perfect in every way – the cars, the crowds, the atmosphere – it truly is 'Glorious Goodwood'.

CLASSICS IN CAMERA

Stig Blomqvist and Audi quattro
PAUL HARMER

Rally legend Stig was reunited with the awesome Audi quattro 25 years after it revolutionised the sport. To celebrate, he blasted this 500bhp S1 down the infamous Col du Turini.

CLASSIC EVENTS

January 24 - 29, 2010

THE WINTER TRIAL
2010 - Austria - Czech Republic - Slovenija - Austria

2010

Register now at www.thewintertrial.eu or mail us at bart.rietbergen@upcmail.nl +31 578 575100

BUENOS AIRES >> RIO DE JANEIRO

CARRERA COPACABANA
2010 - Argentinia - Chile - Peru - Bolivia - Brazil - 2010

2010 live the legend

live the legend...

Oct 23 - Nov 21, 2010

CLASSIC EVENTS

SLRs old and new

Two very different generations
of Mercedes SLR – Sir Stirling

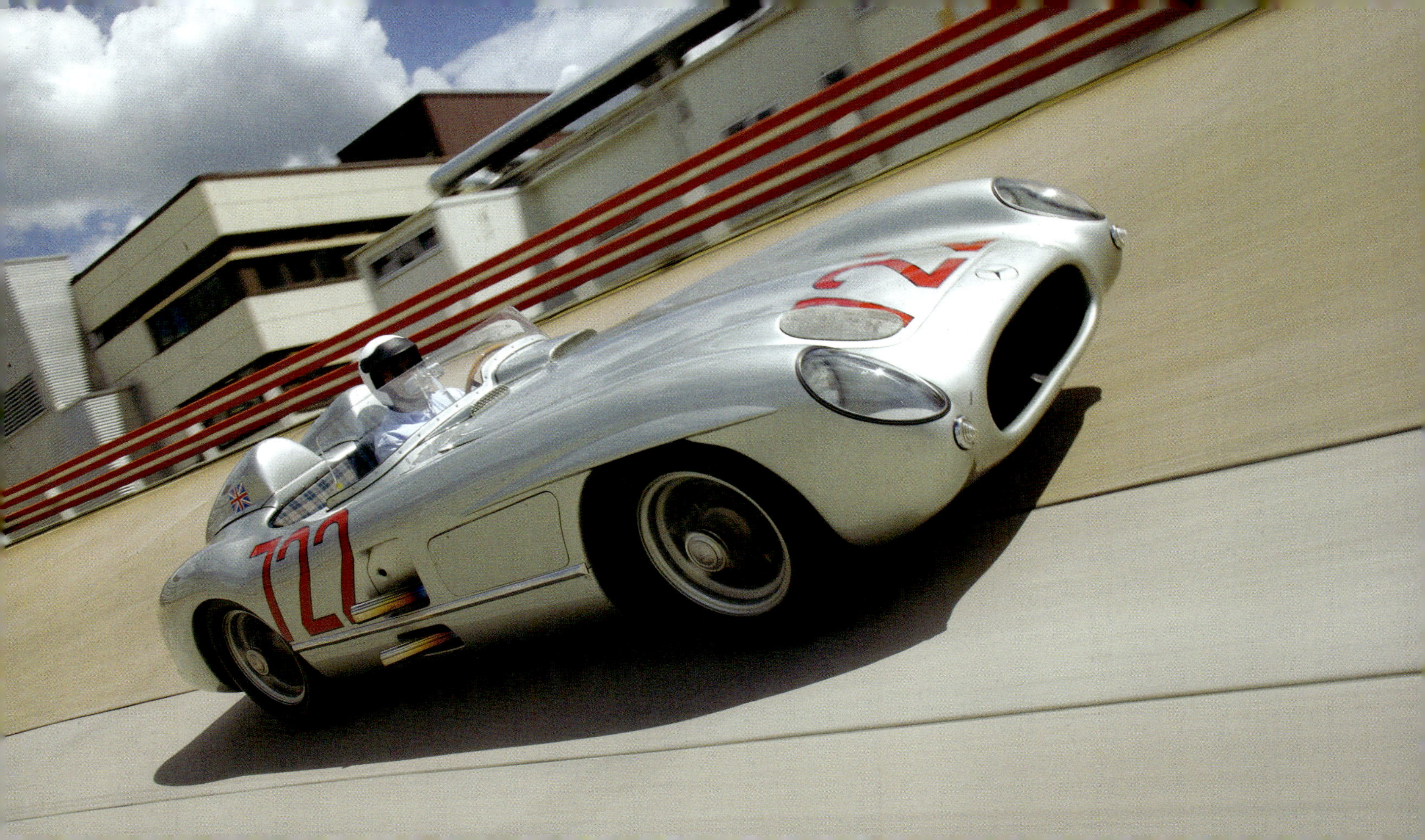
722

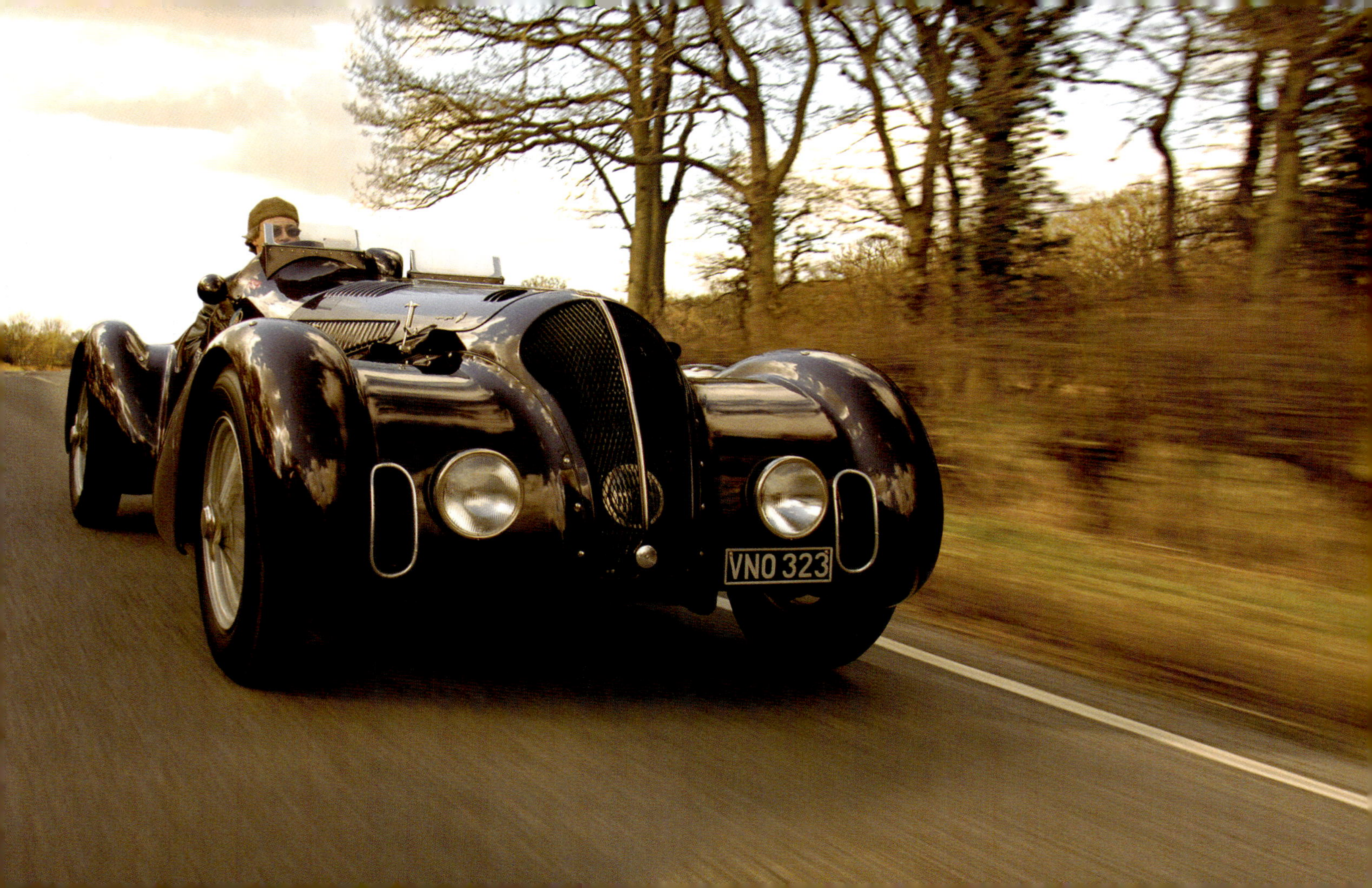
VNO 323

Alfa Romeo
6C 2300B
MICHAEL BAILIE
When we drove it in *Octane*

CLASSICS IN CAMERA

Ford GT40s
MICHAEL BAILIE
Two examples of the Blue Oval's Le Mans legend were brought together in the studio for *Octane* to accompany an in-depth story of the war waged between Ford top brass and their Ferrari counterparts.

CLASSICS IN CAMERA 131

Audi R8
TOM SALT

Audi's modern-day supercar met the ghosts of its successors when *Octane*'s assistant editor Keith Adams drove it to the 'lost circuit' AVUSring in Berlin – 70 years ago home to the fastest racing cars in the world.

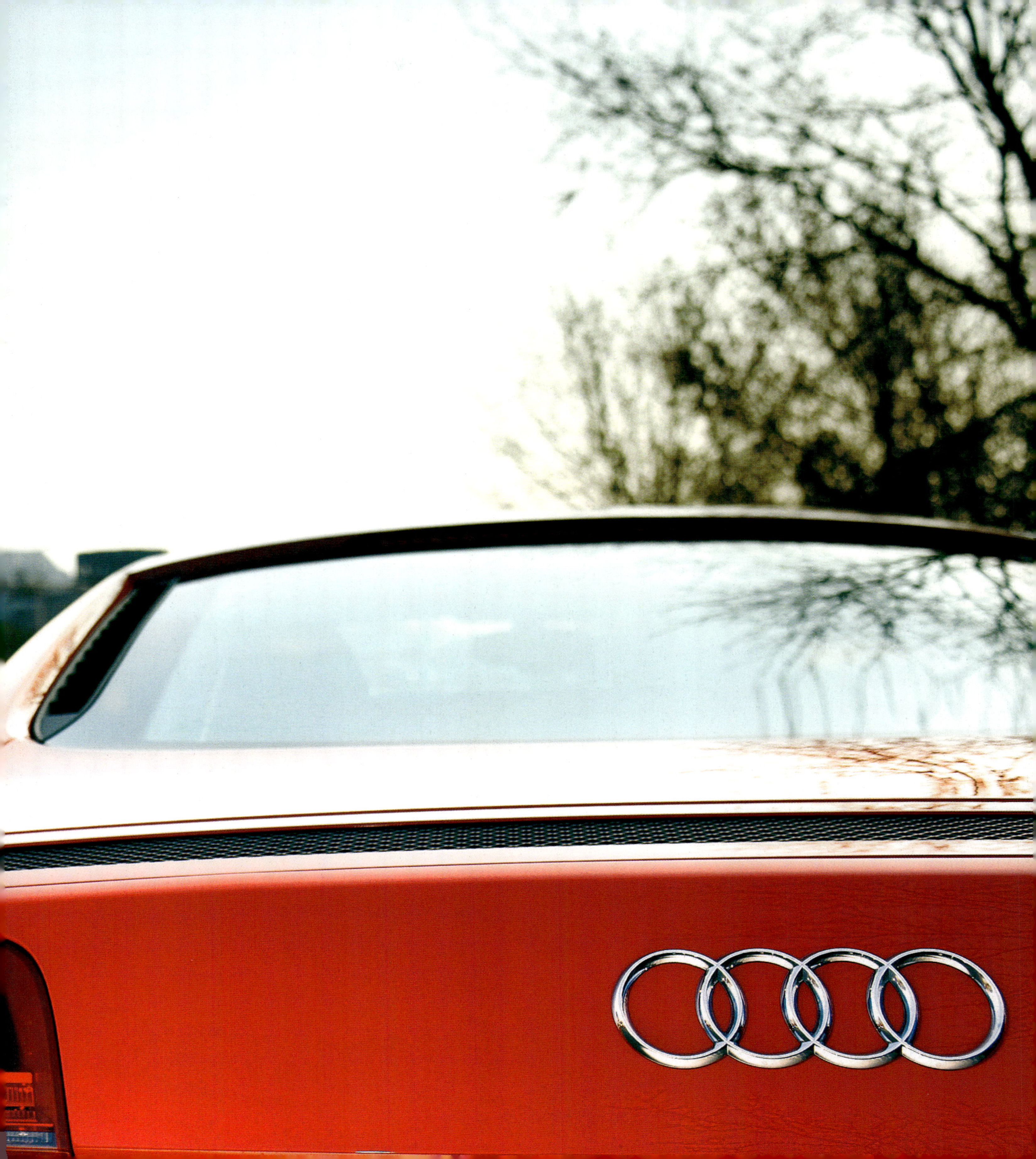

Jaguar XKSS
GEORGE BAMFORD

The E-type is often cited as the most beautiful Jaguar of all time, but its predecessor the XKSS could equally well lay claim to the title. It's basically a race car made road-legal by the addition of a windscreen.

Legendary. Uncompromised. Reborn.

...the XKSS, the ultimate expression of the Jaguar D-type...

Lynx was formed in 1968 and rapidly gained a reputation for the repair and maintenance of specialist sports cars including the legendary racing Jaguar C and D-Types. Over 40 years later, the uncompromising attention to detail and engineering heritage of Lynx continues to hand build exquisite motor cars for collectors and driving enthusiasts throughout the world.

The Lynx XKSS is a painstaking homage to one of the most iconic and exciting sports cars ever built. The spectacular performance and glorious style of Jaguar's past is reborn... today.

Lynx®

T: +44 (0)125 6761 482
E: enquiries@lynxmotors.co.uk
www.lynxmotors.co.uk

CLASSICS IN CAMERA

Mille Miglia
ANTON WATTS

In its original form, this event came to a premature end in 1957 after a tragic accident. Today's version – run over nearly 1000 miles from Brescia to Rome and back – is, in theory at least, more regularity trial than race, but it's still a thrilling challenge.

PRINCIPE & SAVOIA
MILANO
Aix-les-Bains
HÔTEL
REGINA PALACE
RAPALLO
HAFNIA
GRAND HOTEL D'ALBION
AIX-LES-BAINS
GRAND HOTEL
ROYAL
BUDAPEST
ITALIA
PR 20
7521
I

ESTRAL
Roma 15
5501

CLASSICS IN CAMERA

Alfa Romeo BAT 7
ALEX P

Other-worldly bewinged design gives the Bertone-styled BAT 7 – the initials stand for *Berlina Aerodinamica Tecnica* – a back-to-the-future feel. It and its two brothers, BATs 5 and 9, were penned by Franco Scaglione between 1953 and 1955.

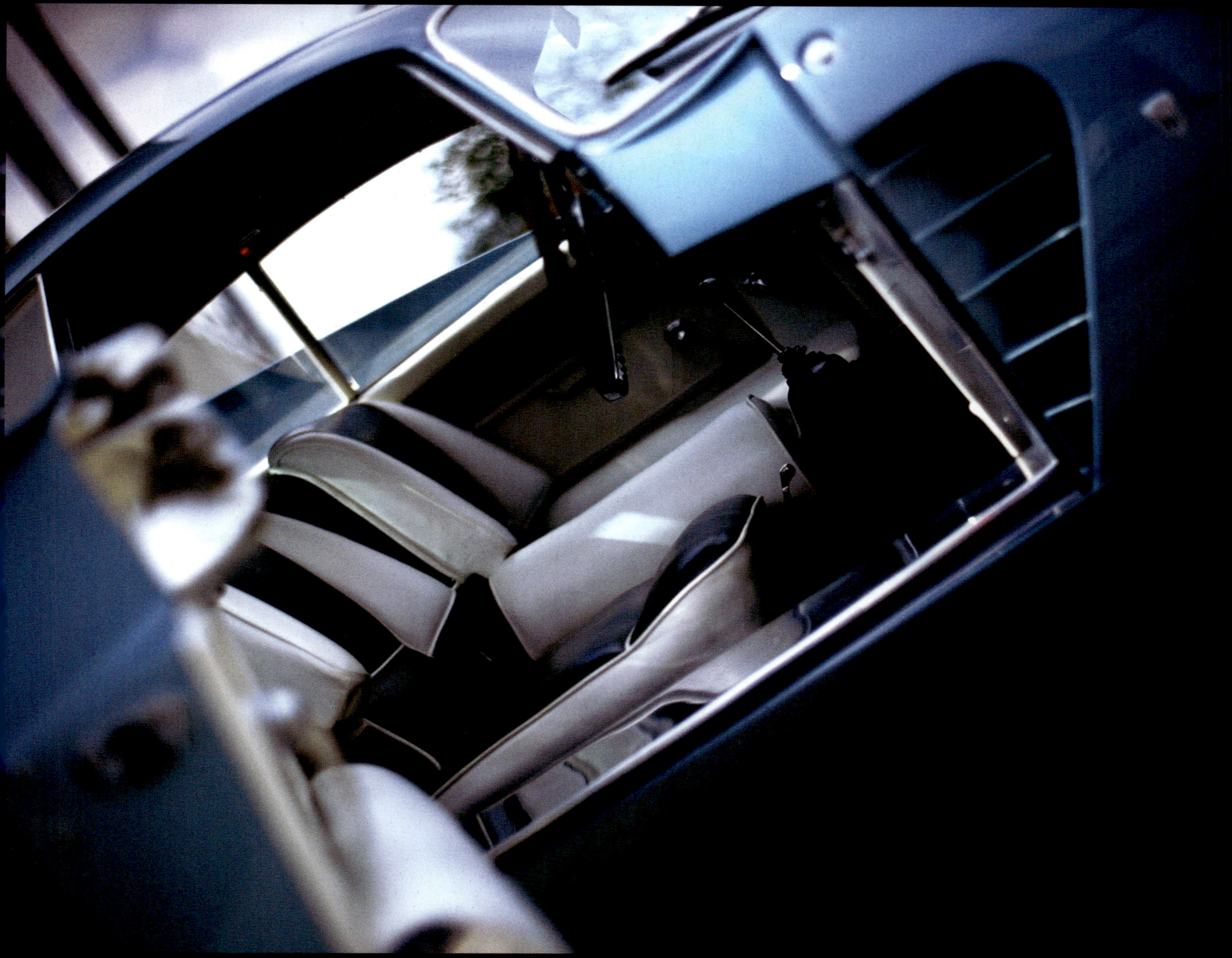

CLASSICS IN CAMERA

Bentley 3 Litre
MATTHEW HOWELL

Contested by May Cunliffe in the 1920s, the supercharged Little Red Bentley anticipated its 4½ 'Blower' stablemates by two years. *Octane* deputy editor Mark Dixon got to grips with its challenging on-road quirks more than eight decades later.

Mercedes-Benz 300SL
LAT
This very original Gullwing started life as a Paris Motor Show star in 1954, before becoming Mercedes-Benz (GB)'s press car and being used by Stirling Moss to reconnoitre the route of the 1955 Mille Miglia.

**Aston Martin
V8 Vantage**
GEORGE BAMFORD
Complete with rocket launchers, windscreen head-up display, retractable skis and spiked tyres, the vehicular star of 007 movie *The Living Daylights* reunited James Bond with an Aston for the first time in 18 years.

CLASSICS IN CAMERA

De Tomaso Panteras
MATTHEW HOWELL

Behind the garage doors of a nondescript suburban home lurks the Pantera collection of Los Angelean Jan Taraszkiewicz. With his orange 1973 Pantera L, red 1973 GT5S conversion from the same year and cranberry 1972 Group 4, he's quite the talk of the neighbourhood!

CLASSICS IN CAMERA

Le Mans Classic
ROD LAWS

With drivers re-enacting the famous Le Mans running start, the 2006 event gets underway. Nearly 400 cars ranging from 1923 to 1979 competed in six classes and 18 races.